PRACTICAL
WOODCARVING

ELEMENTARY AND ADVANCED

TYPICAL EARLY RENASCENCE PANELS, WITH HEADS IN ROUNDELS.
Sixteenth Century, probably French or under French Influence.

PRACTICAL WOODCARVING
ELEMENTARY AND ADVANCED

ELEANOR ROWE

PART I
ELEMENTARY WOOD-CARVING

DOVER PUBLICATIONS, INC.
MINEOLA, NEW YORK

Bibliographical Note

This Dover edition, first published in 2005, is an unabridged republication of *Practical Woodcarving*, comprising two books in one: *Practical Wood-Carving: Elementary Wood-Carving* (Third Edition), published by B.T. Batsford Ltd., London, 1930; and *Practical Wood-Carving: Advanced Wood-Carving* (Second Edition), published by B. T. Batsford Ltd., London, 1930.

Library of Congress Cataloging-in-Publication Data

Rowe, Eleanor.
  Practical wood carving : elementary and advanced / Eleanor Rowe.
    p. cm.
  Reprint. Originally published: London : B.T. Batsford, 1930.
  Includes index.
  ISBN 0-486-44069-9
    1. Wood-carving. I. Title.

NK9704.R6 2005
736'.4—dc22

2004065736

Manufactured in the United States of America
Dover Publications, Inc., 31 East 2nd Street, Mineola, N.Y. 11501

FOREWORD

THE first edition of "Practical Wood-Carving" being exhausted, I have thought it expedient to reissue it in two parts.

The present volume forms part I., "Elementary Wood-Carving," and comprises all the information necessary for a beginner to start carving without the aid of a teacher, as well as the preliminary instruction for high relief carving. It will be found especially useful to those who need an inexpensive manual, and will take the place of my earlier book, "Hints on Wood-Carving" (of which some 19,000 copies were sold), which has long been out of print, yet is still continually asked for.

Part II., "Advanced Wood-Carving," will be published later on. It will contain the remaining chapters of "Practical Wood-Carving," dealing with the carving of Gothic tracery, bosses, finials, and capitals, as well as Renascence details, lettering, &c. The text will be revised, and some fresh illustrations added.

It is hoped that the proposed scheme for starting village industries for disabled soldiers and sailors will take practical form, and that a National School for making simple furniture will be included. For the decoration of such furniture the information given in Chapters IV. and V. of the present volume should be helpful in bringing out the initiative of the student in producing patterns which are the outcome of the tool, whilst the more advanced designer would be able to carry out his design in a simple style of carving.

It is gratifying to know that my books have been a help to the sailors of our Fleet, and I venture to hope the following pages may induce some of those who have suffered in the war to take up the craft as an interesting recreation, and one which might possibly lead, with further training, to a remunerative occupation.

ELEANOR ROWE.

May 1918.

PUBLISHERS' NOTE

THE publishers have to record with deep regret that Miss Eleanor Rowe died on the 3rd of January 1920.

Miss Rowe was attracted in early youth to the study of the Decorative Arts, and she gradually acquired an extensive knowledge of their history through Mediæval and Renascence times. To this she added an intimate study of the greatest artists of all Europe. She was an accomplished, practical craftswoman in several fields of art, and besides being a competent designer, an able illuminator, she was one of the first of her sex to be admitted to the study of architecture; but what most attracted and finally claimed her was the art of carving on wood. She gained the medal of the Society of Arts for wood-carving, and was for many years a member of the Arts and Crafts Society.

Her powers of artistic execution were equalled by her organising ability, and the School of Art of Wood-Carving, where she was a pupil for one year and of which later she was for some years the Manager, largely owes its present assured position and its fine record of useful work to her untiring industry and tactful administration.

Miss Rowe will be known and remembered by her standard works, "Hints on Wood-Carving," "Chip Carving," "Practical Wood-Carving," and the three series, "French Wood-Carving from the National Museums." The present work is a remodelled and extended form of the advanced portions of "Practical Wood-Carving," of which the elementary part was issued separately in 1918. At the time of her death Miss Rowe had completed all necessary arrangements and, fortunately, all that was needed was to see the book through the press.

While it is impossible to help regretting that the indisposition of the last years of Miss Rowe's life prevented her from accomplishing some of the work which lay within her powers, there is no doubt that she will be remembered by the sterling and practical works of which she was the author; and all who had the privilege of fellowship with her realise that her exceptional gifts and great ability were united with a keen and forceful yet altogether charming personality.

The publishers are indebted to Mr W. E. Palmer for permission to reproduce the photograph of Typical Early Renascence Panels which forms the frontispiece to the volume.

CONTENTS

PART ONE

(*Here follows Part 2*)

CLASSIFICATION OF ENGLISH STYLES FROM THE MIDDLE OF THE TWELFTH TO THE EARLY NINETEENTH CENTURY. (*Dates only approximate; included for general guidance.*)

GOTHIC.

EARLY ENGLISH	1150	to	1200	Transition from Norman to Lancet.
	1200	to	1250	Lancet.
DECORATED -	1250	to	1300	Geometrical.
	1300	to	1350	Curvilinear or Flowing.
PERPENDICULAR	1350	to	1450	Perpendicular or Rectilinear.
	1450	to	1525	Tudor.

RENASCENCE.

THE EARLY PERIOD, 1500 to 1640.	1500 to 1550.	The influence of the imported Italian workmen during the reign of Henry VIII.
	Elizabethan, 1550 to 1600. Jacobean, 1600 to 1640.	The influence of the German and Flemish workmen who sought shelter in this country.
THE LATE PERIOD, 1640 to 1820.	Transitional, 1640 to 1660.	The influence of Inigo Jones (1573-1653).
	Late Stuart and Queen Anne, 1660 to 1720.	The influence of Wren (1648-1720). The influence of the French refugees who sought shelter here after the Revocation of the Edict of Nantes in 1683. The Dutch influence under William and Mary.
	Georgian, 1720 to 1760.	The influence of Sir William Chambers (1726-1796) and other Palladian Architects. Interludes of Rococo and Chinoiséne influence.
	Adam, 1760 to 1790.	The influence of the brothers Adam (Robert, 1728-1792). The influence of the later French styles.
	Regency, 1790 to 1820.	The Greek Revival, with later eclecticism.

PRACTICAL WOOD-CARVING

CHAPTER I

THE WOOD-CARVER'S OUTFIT

AT first the beginner had better procure only what is
absolutely necessary. As he proceeds, and finds out
what he wants, he can add to his stock.

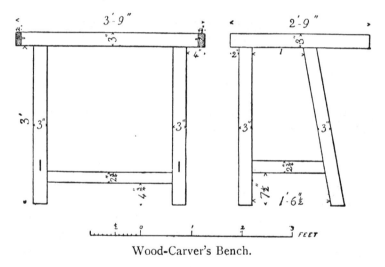

Wood-Carver's Bench.

As no satisfactory work can be done on a table, it
is wiser to start with a good strong bench (see figure).

This bench should be from 3 ft. 2 in. to 3 ft.
5 in. high, and its top or table should be, where space
permits, at least 3 ft. 9 in. by 2 ft. 9 in. wide. It should

I

be made of deal, the two front planks each 3 ft. 6 in. by 11 in. wide and 3 in. thick, with a board at the back of the same length and breadth, but not necessarily of the same thickness, as 1 in. for this would be sufficient. The planks and the board must be secured at the ends with clamps or cleats made of beech, 1½ in. wide by 3 in. thick.

The top should be supported on four legs 3 in. square in section. These must be fixed into the planks so as to secure a strong joint, and the back legs should slope outwards. Into these legs four rails should be strongly morticed, placing the front rail low enough to be a convenient rest for the feet.

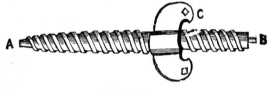

Bench Screw.

If the exigencies of space compel it, the width of the table may be reduced by decreasing the width of the thin board, or this might be omitted altogether. If large work is executed, a good-sized bench is indispensable. The student is advised to try and obtain a second-hand bench, as the price of timber is now so high.

A stool varying in height from 2 ft. 4 in. to 2 ft. 6 in. may be used as an occasional rest ; but it is more workmanlike to stand, and, in the majority of cases, the carver will find that he is obliged to do so. The stools can be procured square or circular, and with cane or wooden seats.

There are various ways of fixing the wood to the bench, but the most popular and by far the most satisfactory is the bench screw (see figure).

Owing to the various positions in which the bench screw is used, one about 8 in. long is found to be the most generally useful. With it is always used a beech block washer about 2½ in. square (see figures 1 and 2), the use of which is to save time in screwing up the nut, as well as to protect the bench from its friction.

C (p. 2) is a butterfly nut, working on the screw AB. Detach it. The rectangular holes on C fit on the projecting point B, whereby C becomes a handle to drive the screw B. Insert the screw at A into the underside of

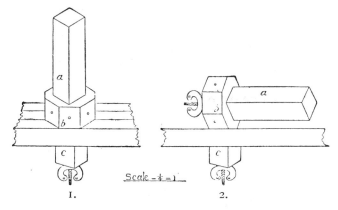

APPLIANCE FOR CARVING IN THE ROUND.

a, Wood to be carved.   b, Octagonal Block.   c, Beech Block Washer.

the board to which your wood is fixed, then pass the point B downwards through a hole provided in the bench, slip on from underneath the beech block, replace C at B and screw up tight and firm (see figure 1, c). If the carver wants to raise his work, a second block may be placed underneath the carving, in the position of the octagon in figure 1, b.

For carving in the round, it is necessary to work on all sides of the wood. Procure an octagonal beech block 2½ in. thick by 6 in. wide, and pierce a hole through the

centre. Slip this over the screw after it has been inserted in the wood which has to be carved (*a*) and secure
it to the bench (p. 3.1). In this vertical position the
wood can be carved on all sides but the base. It is
sometimes necessary to place it horizontally (p. 3.2),
when the second bench screw is required (p. 3.2), and
then we see why the beech block must be octagonal.
It provides eight different flat faces, into each of which
the bench screw can be inserted, each face varying the
position of the work.

The bench screw can only be used with a bench
or with a table in which holes can be made, but when
this is impossible, the student must procure two iron
cramps $4\frac{1}{2}$ in. long, the cost of which is 1s. 9d. each.
For flat low relief work the cramps answer very well,
but for deep or modelled carving, they are most
unsatisfactory.

The " Amateur Portable Bench," which can be fixed
to any table by means of cramps, is convenient for those
who have not a proper bench to work on.

A hold-fast for large work is useful and costs about
7s. 6d. It consists of an iron bar, with a movable arm
hinged on at the top and regulated by a screw. At the
other end of the arm a small iron block with teeth is
hinged on, and this grips the wood. The iron bar is
slipped through a hole in the bench, and the arm is
adjusted to the top of the wood and then screwed down

A vice may sometimes be required, and the most
inexpensive is the ordinary wooden one with a screw
about one and three-quarter inches in diameter. The
wood to be carved is fixed in this, and then the vice is
secured to the bench, either with a bench screw or an
iron cramp.

To keep the tools in good order it is necessary to
have a grindstone. If not used too hard, a hand grind-

stone with a wheel about eight inches in diameter, cost-
ing 8s. 6d., will suffice, but it requires a second person
to turn the wheel. When in use it should be fastened
to the bench by a cramp. A treadle grindstone is better
and quicker although more expensive, and being worked
by the foot no assistance is needed. The prices now
cannot be guaranteed.

In addition to the grindstone, the following list of
things will be necessary :—

A Washita stone for the big tools.

Two or three Arkansas and Turkey stones for the
smaller ones.

A small flat oil-can, filled with the best machine oil,
or with salad oil and a few drops of paraffin.

A strop prepared with emery paste.

A square or round-headed mallet, the latter being
generally preferred (p. 13).

The selection of the tools will depend on the work
to be done and the predilection of the carver, but the
following set of eighteen tools (p. 6) will be found useful
to begin with.

If expense has to be considered, Nos. 1, 12, 15, 16
could be dispensed with at first.

No. 1, the skew or slanting chisel, is used for bevell-
ing or cutting straight lines, also for smoothing the
background of such panels as are free at the edges. A
straight chisel is also handy, but if only one is procured,
the skew chisel is the most useful. These tools are also
known by the name of firmers or corner firmers.

Nos. 2-5, extra flat gouges. These may be procured
in any size from an inch and a half to one-sixteenth of
an inch. They are invaluable for cleaning off the tool
marks, and are much better for this purpose than the
chisel, which is often used, and which produces a far
more mechanical surface. In sending impressions of

these to a tool maker, specify "extra flats," not "chisels," otherwise the latter are sure to be sent.

Nos. 6-11, a variety of gouges used for modelling, fluting, outlining, balls, &c.

Nos. 12, 13, fluters. A technical name given by carvers to very quick gouges; if much bigger than No. 12, they are liable to break. The sizes given are useful for modelling all kinds of foliage, and for *bosting in* work that is varied in its planes.

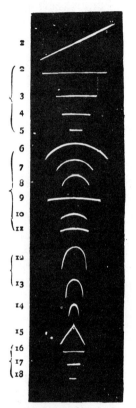

Impressions
of Tools.

No. 14, a veiner, for veined lines, stems, &c., when it would probably be used with the fluters, of which it is a smaller variety.

No. 15, the V-tool. This is a most serviceable and effective tool, but it requires considerable experience to handle properly, is very difficult to sharpen, and soon gets blunt. The same effect can be produced with other tools, and therefore until some dexterity has been obtained, the beginner need not purchase one.

Nos. 16-18, bent background tools. These may be procured from one-sixteenth of an inch and upwards; one larger than three-eighths of an inch is rarely necessary.

Bent gouges or flats are also obtainable, but the student will require some practice before he purchases these.

Fish-tail or spade tools are very useful for finishing,

but they should never be used for *bosting in.* The blade of these tools tapers towards the handle, and consequently it has not the same resisting power as the ordinary tool. For chip-carving, a spade chisel is more handy than the ordinary chisel.

The router, very similar to the tool called by the joiner an "old woman's tooth," may occasionally be used. It consists of a small chisel, inserted into a piece of wood, and the chisel is fixed by means of a wedge, to the depth of the relief required. An opening is made with a tool in the middle of one of the ground spaces of the panel to be carved, and the router is then inserted and worked backwards and forwards until the required depth is reached. Students, however, should be able to make a clean level ground before attempting to use the router. It should never be relied on for finishing the ground, but as a gauge to test the depth is useful. A match inserted in a card or thin piece of wood will answer the purpose of a measure. The student, however, should bear in mind that a perfectly level smooth ground, which gives the appearance of the carved detail being applied, is not to be desired. A judicious variation in the level of the ground is a very great advantage. Various fancy tools are made, in which the Macaroni tool would be included. Very few practical woodcarvers ever use them.

A list of the various makers, with the prices of the tools, is given at the end of the book.

New tools, as a rule, take longer to sharpen than those which have been used. After a little practice, the student will soon see, according to the work that he undertakes, what tools he requires, therefore it is better to buy only a few at first, and add to them as experience dictates. Never buy a tool maker's assorted set, as the experience of a carver is needed to know what tools will be the most useful. Also beware of "Ladies' Sets!" If women are to do good work, they should use the same tools as a man.

Students who sharpen their own tools will soon see the necessity of careful handling, and will not knock them about or dig them into the bench, as the novice invariably does. It is not a good plan to put the points of the tools in cork, as it is often damp and rusts the steel.

Tools easily get damaged, and are best kept in a green baize case when not in use.

Glass-paper must on no account be used on the carving. The student should from the first aim at a sharp steady cut, and should never have recourse to glass-paper or a file to make good a bad cut. Glass-paper not only spoils the texture of the wood, but it destroys the delicate details of the carving, by which the carver expresses his feeling in his work.

Without sharp tools good work is impossible. To keep the tools sharp, and in good order, is economy of time.

No tool maker can be depended upon to send tools out sharpened to the nicety that is required. Nor is it wise to entrust them to a carpenter, as they are sharpened quite differently to a carpenter's tools, and require a delicate and special handling. So the sooner a student learns how to sharpen his tools for himself, the better for him.

The implements are—the grindstone, which is a revolving stone; the Washita, the Turkey, and the Arkansas stones; some slips with curved edges for the inner side of curved tools; and the leather strop.

The first step is to adjust the convex edges of the slips to fit the concave inner edge of the curved tools. For this purpose get three sheets of glass-paper, Nos. o,

1, and middle 2. The coarse paper, No. 2, removes more of the stone than the fine paper, but, if the slips are very thick, it is better to use the grindstone. Take a small block of wood and stretch a piece of glass-paper over it. Hold this in your left hand and the slip in your right, and rub the slip first on the one side and then on the other till you have ground it down into the required curve.

The Treadle Grindstone.

Always finish off with the fine paper, No. 0, as you must have the edges delicately smooth. Be careful to remove all the grit before using the stones for the tools.

The grindstone is used for the rougher and heavier work.

Tools should always be purchased ground and ready for use, although even under these conditions each carver has to adjust them to his own requirements.

If the cutting edge of a tool shows any irregularities, such as a white line or a speck, or an unequal or angular surface where the tool has been ground, it will generally be necessary to use the grindstone, although if the in-

equalities are very slight, the Washita stone, wetted
with oil, may be sufficient.   The white line or speck
shows that the steel has been left too thick.   In getting
rid of this thickness the grindstone must be used with
plenty of water to prevent the steel from becoming hot
enough to interfere with the tempering.   The illustration
(p. 9) shows how the tool should be held : the right hand
grasps the handle, holding the tool sloping slightly up-

Grinding the Edge of a Broken Tool.

wards at an angle of about 30° to the stone, while the
forefinger of the left hand presses the edge, and keeps
it down in even and firm contact.   The stone is revolved
away from the tool and as rapidly as possible.   The
tool, meanwhile, is steadily moved from margin to
margin, right across the stone, thus shifting its position
in order to prevent forming grooves in it.   Tools that
have not previously been ground are done in the same
way, but they take a much longer time.

The grindstone is necessary when tools are broken or jagged. In this case the end of the tool must be held against the grindstone in the manner shown in the illustration (p. 10), and ground until the line of the tool is restored. After that it must be held against the

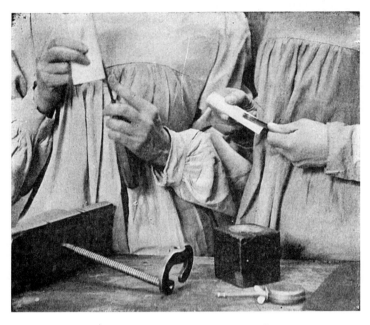

A.

B.

Using the Washita Stone for the
Inside of the Tool.

Using the Washita Stone for the
Outside of the Tool.

grindstone and worked from side to side as has previously been described (p. 10).

Never use a tool straight from the grindstone. The grindstone must always be followed by the use of the slip and the strop in the manner hereafter described.

In the case of the curved edged tools the stones and slips are held in the right hand, and are rubbed briskly against the tools, which are held in the left hand. The proper way of holding them is shown in the illustration (p. 11). The stone or slip is held with the fingers of the right hand at the back of it, and the thumb in front, but as near the edge as possible to avoid danger from a slip of the tool. The left arm and elbow should rest firmly against the body, while the hand holds the tool as shown in the illustrations, accordingly as the flat or the convex edge of the stone is being made use of. The stone and tool must be held slanting upwards, so that the cutting edge can easily be seen. The tool must press against the stone firmly, and the stone must be moved briskly.

The sharpening process begins with the convex back of the curved tools (p. 11, B). This is first laid against the stone, and gently and evenly turned on its axis from side to side, so that the whole sweep of the curve is brought evenly in contact with the stone. The pressure should be even, but a little more may be put on parts that appear thicker ; but too much pressure will produce angles at the back, and these should be carefully avoided. When the back appears satisfactory, take a slip that exactly fits the concavity of the tool and rub it smartly up and down, using the lower part of the slip, and keeping it as flat as possible, so as not to turn the edge (p. 11, A).

Great care must be taken to make the back of the tool take the same sweep of curve as the front. It should be quite smooth and free from angles, and no bevel of any sort, however slight, should be perceptible on either back or front.

Having finished with the slip, wipe the tool with a rag, and then strop it on the leather (see figure B opposite). Hold the tool firmly in the right hand, with the forefinger on the blade, keeping it just sufficiently flat to catch the edge without turning it, and draw the back of the tool quickly and firmly down the leather—the quicker and the firmer the better. Lastly the inside must be stropped. When the tool is curved the leather should be bent over the finger. For this reason it is better not to have the leather glued to a board, which is sometimes recommended.

The tool should be tested by cutting a piece of pinewood across the grain, and should be considered satisfactory only if it cuts as sharply as a razor. If one side

A.

B.

Sharpening a Chisel.   Stropping the Tool.

cuts better than the other, the stone must be used again, more pressure being applied to the faulty side. Care must be taken to keep the corners of the tool square. The cutting edge must be straight and not curved— this ⌐⌐, not that ⌒.

The straight edged tools—the chisel and skew chisel —are sharpened somewhat differently (see figure A). The Washita oil-stone rests on the bench without moving, and the tool, with its handle kept very low, is rubbed up and down it, first on one side and then on the other till the edge is sufficiently thin. The tool must be kept rigidly and evenly flat against the stone. The process is completed by the use of the strop. Some carvers like one side of the chisel with a longer bevel than the other, but this is a point each must decide for himself.

The V tools and small veiners are very difficult to sharpen. Each side of the V (or parting) tool must be ground and sharpened like the chisel, but the inside requires great care, and a slip shaped like a wedge must be used. The stropping may be done on the edge of the leather, or a small piece of hard wood may be cut to fit the tool, and covered with a little emery-paste and rubbed inside. The student should not attempt to grind these tools until he has had considerable practice with the others. Tools for soft woods require a longer bevel and must be ground thinner than for hard woods like oak and walnut. For ebony and rosewood the bevel must be quite short.

The strop should be in constant use, as by this means tools are kept to a keen edge. It should be kept in brown paper or some stout covering to protect it from dust and grit.

The slips should be wiped before they are put away. When carving, the tools should be placed on the bench in front of the carver with the handles towards him, and arranged in gradation according to the various sweeps of the tool. Only those likely to be required for the work in hand should be put out.

The foregoing instructions and suggestions are meant only for the beginner. When dexterity is obtained, various ways and means suggest themselves to the expert which it would be unwise for the novice to attempt.

Border, with initials and date, suitable for carving.—J. G. E.

CHAPTER II

THE VARIOUS WOODS USED BY THE CARVER

ALL woods for carving should be close grained, well seasoned, and with as little figure as possible. " Figure " is the technical name for the dark wavy lines that may be seen on the surface of olive-wood, maple, bird's-eye maple, and some kinds of Italian walnut. In oak it is much more marked and is called the " silver grain," but for carving the less of this the better.

Oak is the most popular wood used by the carver, and from its durability, and the beautiful colour it gets by age, is likely to retain its popularity.

There are several kinds of oak, the best being of native growth, and next to this the Austrian oak. American oak is coarser, and not fit for good work. Wainscot oak should be avoided by the carver, as it has too much figure and is very hard.

Chestnut closely resembles oak without the " silver grain," it is not so tough, and is very unequal, but when good it has much to recommend it. It is more likely to get worm-eaten than oak.

Walnut is imported from various places. The American is on the whole the best, if carefully chosen with a close even grain and not too much figure. English walnut is tougher and not easy to get; when good it is quite suitable for carving.

Italian walnut is an excellent wood, closer grained and harder than the American or the English walnut, and, though not so dark, is a beautiful bronze colour and cuts well. It should be selected free from black streaks, but is not now easily procured.

Satin-walnut is an inferior wood and not so expensive. It is lighter in colour than the others, but is very uncertain in the way it cuts.

Mahogany is an ugly red colour, but it is good for carving, especially for work that has to be painted or gilded.

Rosewood and ebony are difficult to carve, being so hard and gritty that they turn the edges of the tools. Carvers should avoid using them if possible, but when necessity compels it the design should be considered with special regard to the material.

It is surprising that teak is not more used in England for carving. There are several kinds, and some very hard, but that which is imported from Burmah is said to be the best. It is durable and not easily affected by damp. It cuts well and is a nice colour, and for this reason is most suitable for the panelling of rooms, doors, chests, &c. It is quite the best wood to use for any carved monument to be placed out of doors. The wood work in Truro Cathedral is of teak. Oak, with all its advantages, is too light in colour when new; and although it can be fumigated, this adds to the expense, and the wood loses some of its vigour in the process. Teak requires to be selected, as some of the planks have numerous black streaks, which spoil the effect of the carving as well as the colour. At the present time the right kind of teak for carving is not very plentiful.

The Australian jarreh-wood is a beautiful red, a little coarse in the grain, and though hard cuts fairly well, but the tools must not be too thin. Boxwood, pearwood, sandalwood, and satinwood are best suited to figures and fine, delicate work ; boxwood is, however, very hard and very scarce.

Lime and holly are soft and even in the grain, but being light in colour they require staining or gilding. American bass-wood is a fairly good wood, but variable, and sometimes gritty. It is cheaper than lime, not nearly so nice to carve, and can rarely be used for fine work.

Sycamore is a white wood, and is suitable for bread platters, bowls, and butter trays. It is tough and rather difficult to cut, as it contains a slight amount of sand, which is apt to blunt the tools.

Lime is the best wood for chip-carving. Holly and sycamore are also suitable but harder, and consequently more difficult to cut.

Several kinds of pine are good for carving, but deal should be avoided. Pitch pine is excellent for work exposed to the weather, but disagreeable to carve, from being very sticky. The student cannot do better than begin his studies with yellow pine, but must be careful to get only the best quality, there being cheaper varieties which are quite unsuitable. Carpenters rarely keep the best. Yellow pine needs careful working, as it is soft, and easily splits, and requires very sharp tools to make clean cuts. This makes it most excellent practice ; for when once the student has mastered these difficulties he will find that he can model with infinitely greater freedom than if he had confined himself to the far less plastic hard woods. The work of all beginners is apt to be hard and mechanical. It is most instructive to compare the carving of amateurs who have worked only in oak, walnut, or other hard woods, with that of others who have had a sound elementary training in pine. The difference is remarkable. The first amateurs have remained cramped and stiff in their work, the second have attained to freedom and breadth.

Kauri pine does not cut quite so well as the yellow pine, but being tougher does not indent so easily. It can be stained readily, and has many points to recommend it.

A carpenter or joiner usually calls wood "stuff," and the dimensions are taken before the wood is planed. What is called 1-in. stuff would when planed be rather less than the inch. The ordinary wood for cabinet work is sold in planks or boards by the timber merchant.

A plank is from 2 to 4 in. thick, and a board is anything under 2 in.

Yellow pine is only sold in planks. They are usually about 12 to 14 ft. long by about 9 to 12 in. wide by 3 in. thick. This thickness can be reduced at the timber yard as required, by sawing the plank longitudinally.

For ordinary work it is a good plan to order one plank with "two cuts"; you will then get three boards each a little under the 1 in. thick, the saw cut slightly reducing the thickness of the wood.

When ordering a panel, the grain of the wood should run the long way of the panel, and the greatest measurement should be put first, thus—14 in. by 6 in. by 1 in., the last figure standing for the thickness of the wood.

The panel to be carved should be glued to a rough deal board about 1 in. thick; this must be quite level, but not too smoothly planed. The glue must be quite hot, and should be lightly applied in spots here and there to the two pieces of wood, and these should be placed afterwards under a weight for an hour or more.

Unless the carved panel is securely fixed to the board, it continually comes off, and not only causes annoyance, but delay.

To separate the carved panel from the board, insert a chisel or an old knife at intervals round the sides, and gently raise the one from the other, until they come apart. Force must not be used, but a tap on the chisel with the mallet may sometimes be necessary. The carpenter or joiner can remove any superfluous glue from the back of the panel when completing the work.

Section of Wooden Clip, with Screw.

When working with cramps it is not necessary to glue the wood to be carved to a board, this is only required for the bench screw. It is very much nicer than the cramps, as it enables the carver to shift his work to any position.

When glue is not available the wood may be fixed to the board with small iron or wooden clips (see figure), or three or four brass buttons, similar to those used on cupboard doors ; sometimes large brass-headed pins can be utilised.

Fifteenth-Century Miserere, Etchingham.

Detail from top rail of an old oak chest, English.
From "Carved Oak Woodwork." W. Bliss Sanders.

CHAPTER III

CONSTRUCTION

THE amateur experiences some difficulty in finding suitable objects, not too ambitious, as a field for his carving. I propose in this chapter to give the construction of a few simple pieces of domestic furniture. They

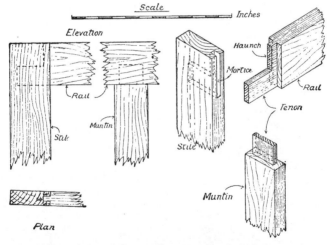

Constructional Members in Framing.

could be made by any country joiner, and could be carved by anyone with a moderate amount of technical skill.

Before proceeding, it will be as well to explain some of the technical terms used.

Panels are set in a frame composed of rails and stiles, and sometimes muntins. The outside vertical members are called " stiles." The inside vertical members separating two or more panels in the same frame are known as " muntins." The horizontal members go by the name of " rails." These various members are morticed and tenoned together. An elevation and plan is given of an ordinary piece of framing on

I.
Mitre Joint.

the previous page. On the right of this, the mortice and tenon joint is shown in isometric projection. The mortice is cut in the stile and a haunch tenon on the end of the rail; this fits into the mortice. The haunch tenon is generally used at the angles, and the simple tenon used for interior joints. The muntin carries the tenon, and the rail has the mortice into which the tenon fits. The thickness of the tenon should be one-third of the thickness of the wood; the width of it not more than five times its thickness. The tenon may be any length, provided in cabinet work it does not go through the stile into which it is morticed. When the ordinary mortice and tenon joint is used, the abutting surfaces of the wood are brought together square.

2. A Tongue in Mitre Joint.

For mouldings, on account of their varied planes, a square joint is impossible. The wood is then cut at an angle of 45°, and is described as a mitre joint. The simplest form of this is shown in Fig. 1.

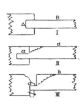

3. Section of Panels in their Frame Posts.

After the two pieces of wood have been cut and glued together, a fine saw cut is made in the outer angle, in a direction at right angles to the mitre line (figure 2). Into the triangular slot, so made, is glued a thin triangular slip of wood (*a*) which serves as a tongue to unite the sides and strengthen the mitre joint. There are various ways of preparing the panel for carving, the simplest being when it is squared at the edges (p. 21.3, 1).   B is the face of the panel.   A groove is made in the framing, into which the panel is fitted. For low relief work, when the framing is simple and of slight projection, this is the method usually employed for chests and ordinary cabinetmaker's work.

If the panel is more than $\frac{3}{8}$ in. thick, it should then be rebated all round to the depth of the ground, as at *a*, II.   It is then inserted into a groove in the framing, as above described.   The reason for rebating the panel is to bring the surface of the carving forward.   When the carving is elaborate, the framing is usually moulded, as III., or it may have a somewhat bolder projection.   In this case the rebate is cut in the frame, deeper than the rebate in the panel, into which the panel can be placed. A wooden beading is then laid all round in the angle, between the back of the carving and the edge of the frame.   This beading, or any applied moulding, must be pinned to the frame; it must not be pinned to the panel, as that would in time cause the panel to split.

The object of the framing is to keep the panel from twisting, and it also enables the joiner to use thinner stuff, and to make his work lighter.   Unframed panels, such as are used for blotters, &c., are liable to become distorted.

Wood will shrink even when it is framed, but to avoid splitting, the panel should be left free with plenty of play.

The cabinetmaker's work must first be fitted together. It is then taken to pieces by him, and all the parts which are to be carved are placed in the carver's hands.   When the carving is completed, the various pieces are returned to the cabinetmaker, who will then put the whole finally together.

The student should never begin, as is so often done, by carving the details before the construction has been carefully considered and drawn out. The construction and the decoration of it must be thought out together if good proportion and harmony are to be attained. Unless the student has some knowledge of the way the wood is put together, he is liable to spoil his work by cutting into the joints.

I once saw a piece of panelling ruined through ignorance of the construction. The student had carved a border of Gothic tracery on the framing, and had taken the ground down too low, so that the mortice and tenon joints had been cut into. This was not only very unsightly, but the requisite strength was gone. Repeating patterns in which little or no ground is removed are the most suitable for this purpose, but they should be used with discretion, as the value of plain surfaces must not be lost sight of.

The front of an old French coffer is given on p. 67 ; as it is only a fragment, I propose here to show how it may be completed.

The front and side elevation of the chest is given on p. 24, figures 1 and 2, with a section through the centre of the front. It shows the panel rebated and let into a groove in the rails. The small square sinkings at a are run out by the joiner's plane.

The stiles are 5 in. wide, and $1\frac{3}{8}$ in. thick, and the thickness of these might be increased by half an inch.

The lid (figure 3) is $\frac{3}{4}$ in. thick, and has a clamp of wood a at either end, to keep the wood from twisting. The pattern for the lid has been adapted from the top rail ; it must be set out free of the clamps, as well as of the tongue which unites the two together.

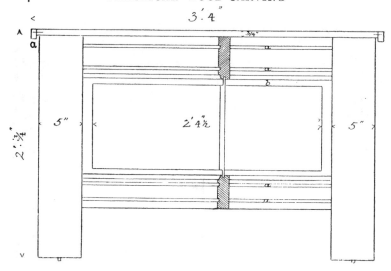

1. Front Elevation.

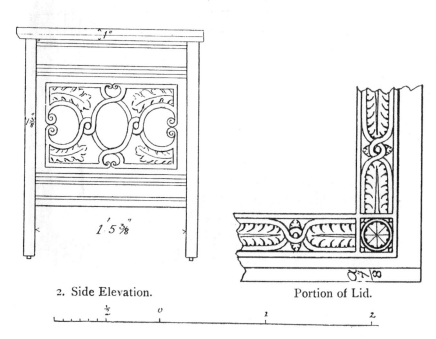

2. Side Elevation.   Portion of Lid.

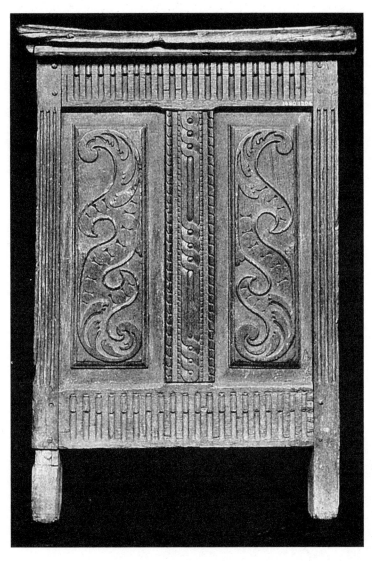

END OF COFFER (p. 26).
Height, 2 ft. 3 in. ; width, 1 ft. 8 in. No. 1480-1904.

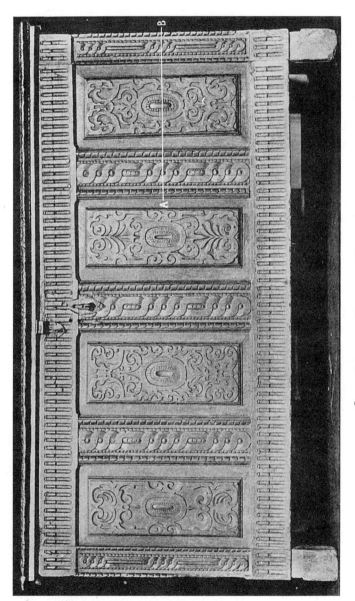

OAK COFFER, FRENCH (FRONT).
Second half of Sixteenth Century; height, 2 ft. 3 in.; width, 4 ft. 8¾ in.
Victoria and Albert Museum, No. 1480-1904.

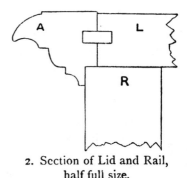

2. Section of Lid and Rail,
half full size.

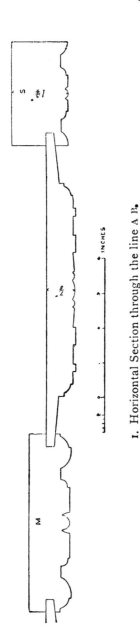

1. Horizontal Section through the line A B.

The design for the end panels
is part of the design of the front.
This chest works out very well
in teak.

The chest opposite is composed of four panels in the
front, the sight measure of the
carving being 15 by 5¼ in., divided by three muntins 5 in.
wide, with a stile at either end
3 in. wide, and a fluted and
reeded rail top and bottom,
4 in. wide.

A section is given on the
line AB, which will explain
the construction. (1) The stiles
and muntins have a mould-
ing at the edges, and the rails
are stop-chamfered on the inside
—that is to say, the chamfer is
stopped before reaching the
muntins, on account of the
mortice and tenon joint. The
edge of the carved panel is

finished off with a small quarter-round moulding, and then a bevel which is let into a groove in the framing. The moulding and the bevel should be done by the cabinetmaker before the panel is carved. The strapwork on the panel is barely ⅛ in. in relief, and is kept flat and not modelled. The carving of the flutes and of the mouldings is described in Chapter IV. The construction of the lid differs from that on p. 24. Instead of the clamps at either end, the front and sides of the lid are framed in with a moulding which is mitred at the angles.

A section is given through the centre of the lid and of the top rail (p. 27.2).

A shows the mouldings which frame in the lid. The thumb moulding, and hollow underneath it, only remain of the old work ; the other mouldings, the ovolo and hollow shown in section, are a suggested restoration. L is the lid, and the little tongue between the lid and the moulding is inserted to hold the two together. R is a part of the top rail.

Below the bottom rail in both these French chests there has evidently been another member, but no traces remain of either of them now.

A charming piece of simple furniture is the French stool. The seat is moulded, and a band of wood, about 6 in. deep and ¾ in. thick, runs along the front and back ; it helps to keep the carved ends in position.

A front elevation is given of the stool on p. 30, and on the right of this, a section on the line AB. The sections of the moulding of the seat, and of the longitudinal pieces of wood that run along the front and back, are shaded, as well as the section of the turned rails ; these are a modern restoration. By substituting for the rails a shelf, which could be grooved into the ends, a small table or "what-not" could be made. In this case it would be unnecessary to plant on the

WALNUT STOOL (FRENCH).
Second half of Sixteenth Century.   Victoria and Albert Museum,
No. 513-1897.

small circular discs which cover over the rails, but in place of them, ornamental pateræ or rosettes, might be carved out of the solid. If the circular ornaments were omitted altogether, the design would not be properly balanced. The moulding of seat could be carved similarly to that given on p. 48.

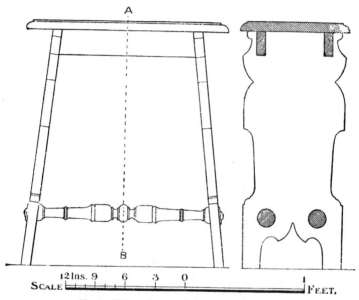

Front Elevation and Section of Stool.

The wood to be carved should be shaped to the outline of the section.

The panelling on the opposite page, though crudely carved, is full of suggestive detail. The rails are plain, except where the lower edge of the panel abuts against the surface of the rail, and then it is stop-chamfered (p. 27), a survival of the Gothic weathering.

The muntins are moulded, the vertical treatment giving the effect of great stability to the framing. The

OAK PANELLING FROM A HOUSE AT WALTHAM ABBEY, ESSEX.
English ; First half of Sixteenth Century. Victoria and Albert Museum, No. 2011-1899.

carved panels abound in the "tool cut" patterns fully
dealt with in the next chapter. They help to illustrate
the value of these enrichments on simple carving, such
as the bands of the circles, the scrolls, and the vases.

The design is typical of the early Renascence, in
which medallions form a conspicuous feature, and in

Side Elevation

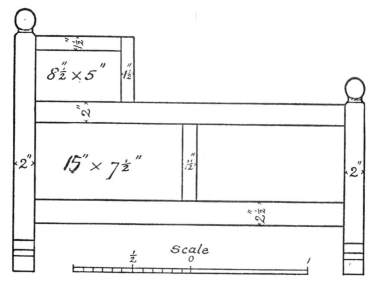

Working Drawings of a Seventeenth-Century Cradle.

which some Gothic detail may often be traced, as the
chamfer to the panels and the arch, and the finial in the
example from St Cross (p. 39).

This panelling is said to have formed part of the
decoration of the Abbey House at Waltham Abbey,
which was granted at the dissolution of the monasteries
by Henry VIII. to Sir Anthony Denny. The Tudor
rose, the portcullis and pomegranate of Catharine of

Arragon, as well as the arms of Denny, are repeated several times on the panelling.

The working drawings are measured from an old cradle dated 1687. In the original there is a group of mouldings worked on the rails, stiles, and muntins, where the panels are inserted. For the mouldings the width of the frame should be slightly increased.

Various ways of preparing the panel have already been given. One of the most satisfactory would be a $\frac{3}{4}$ in. chamfer leaving a square edge to panel about $\frac{1}{16}$ in. in the manner of the French chest (p. 26), omitting the small ovolo moulding.

I.

Elevation at head

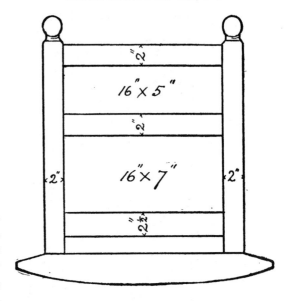

Elevation at foot

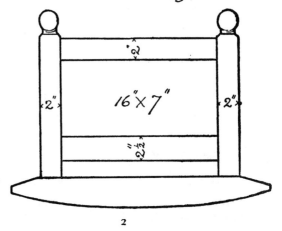

2

Working Drawings of a Seventeenth-Century Cradle.

Suggestions for patterns will be found in Chapters
IV., V., and VI. The relief should be rather less than

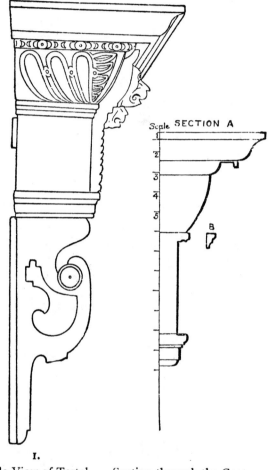

Scale SECTION A

B

I.

Side View of Towel   Section through the Centre
     Roller.   of Towel Roller.

$\frac{1}{8}$ in. Simple construction does not lend itself to elaborate ornamentation, which would be quite out of place
on such an object. The knobs should be left plain, so

that there should be no unequal surface to cause friction to the hand.

The frame is out of 1-in. stuff, the panel $\frac{1}{2}$ in., the rockers $1\frac{1}{2}$ in. The stiles are 2 in. square, and the circular knobs at the end would be turned out of this.

CASE FOR TOWEL ROLLER.

Carved Oak, with Deep Projecting Cornice. English. Second half of Seventeenth Century. Height, 2 ft. 1 in.; width, 2 ft. 3 in.; depth, 10 in. Victoria and Albert Museum, No. 1,200-1875.

The framework could be carved with the gouge-cut patterns given in the next chapter, excepting B, p. 49, which would be too deep. The carving on the panel should be simple, and the chamfer round it wide, so as to reduce the carved surface. Carved surfaces are much more effective when not brought too close together. A monogram and date could be introduced in the panel and on the rail at the foot.

If the upper panels at the head and the rockers were omitted, and the stiles made all the same height, an additional two or three inches being added at the base, an excellent box for logs of wood could be made. The addition of a lid would give a well-proportioned small chest.

The Jacobean towel roller is an admirably designed piece of simple furniture, although the carving is somewhat rude and the masks very ugly.   Section A, p. 34.2, gives the mouldings above the roller, and B is the small carved moulding at the base. The front part of the frieze between the leaf brackets could be made to open by fitting a revolving hinge on the right side, and a small wooden or brass knob on the left side for the handle. The interior space could then be utilised for soap, brushes, &c.

For the construction of simple English furniture the student cannot do better than refer to " Examples of Carved Oak Woodwork of the Sixteenth and Seventeenth Centuries," and " Half-Timbered Houses and Carved Oak Furniture of the Sixteenth and Seventeenth Centuries," by the late W. Bliss Sanders.

These books can be consulted in the Library of the Victoria and Albert Museum on payment of 6d. for a weekly ticket.

A fine example is given on the opposite page of a seventeenth-century late Jacobean chest, the design of the upper rail being much more elaborate than is to be found in the earlier work of that century. The construction is practically the same as the large French coffer, but the lid is clamped as in the smaller French example (pp. 24, 26).

It will be noted that in the large chests, muntins

Late Seventeenth-Century English Chest, in the possession of Mrs W. Bliss Sanders.

have to be used in order that the size of the panel may be reduced, but when this is not necessary (p. 67) they have been dispensed with.

In making a design for a picture frame, when a mitred joint (p. 21) is employed, due regard must be given to the mitre. This handicaps the designer very much, and what is usually done is to have a leaf at the angle with a raised stem, so as to contain the mitre without cutting into it.

In designing the construction for a carved box, the plinth or base on which the side rests should project beyond the lid and be fairly thick. The sides of the box can be mitred and tongued or dovetailed together, the latter being the best method but the most expensive. The margin should be arranged to cover the joints (p. 74). The space for the lock and key must also be considered and the design made with this in view.

Bellows are prepared in three pieces of wood. The back in one piece, with a hole in the centre for the wind, and the front in two pieces. After these are carved they are hinged together with a piece of leather.

The wood is prepared differently for a pipe nozzle to when a clip nozzle is selected, so that point ought to be decided before the carving is begun.

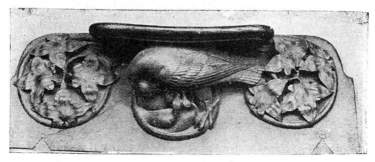

Fourteenth-Century Miserere, Wells.

Carved Oak Canopy over a stall in a side chapel of the Church
of Saint Cross, Winchester.   English (?).   First half of
Sixteenth Century.

Fourteenth-Century Miserere, Wells.

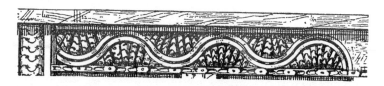

Part of rail and stile of an oak chest, English.
(?) Sixteenth century.

CHAPTER IV

THE OUTCOME OF THE TOOL

THE aim of this chapter is to point out to the student how much he may learn from the tool, and that by understanding a few simple cuts, the endless variety of patterns he may make.

It is therefore advisable that the student should, before he begins to carve, try each one of his tools in turn so as to find out the various cuts they produce, as well as to gain facility in the hand-ling of them (see pp. 64, 65).

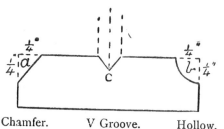

Chamfer.   V Groove.   Hollow.

For this purpose procure a piece of the best yellow pine, with a pencil gauge a line a quarter of an inch from the outside edge all round the top sur-face of the panel and on the side (p. 87). Three or four extra lines beyond these may be put in for further practice. An H or HH pencil is the best for marking lines on the wood. The section annexed gives a chamfer moulding at *a*, a hollow moulding at *b*, and a V groove moulding at *c*. The dotted lines at the corners show the wood before the mouldings are cut. A chisel or a skew chisel is the right tool to use for the chamfer, but failing either of these, take the flattest tool of the set, and proceed to cut away the wood as shown at *a*. It is better at first to keep within the pencilled lines, as when finished the angle produced by the cut should be true. If the panel is large it is impossible to cut the chamfer or run the hollow with one sweeping cut, so it is better to commence with short cuts, and gradually increase them as dexterity is obtained.

Various sized gouges according to the width desired are used for the hollow mouldings, and these are easier to do if the angle of the wood is previously chamfered. This applies to all mouldings done by hand (Chapter VI., pp. 69.2, 71).

Having practised the chamfers and the hollows, next proceed to the V groove. To do this three lines, *c*, 1, and 2, one-eighth of an inch apart, must be set out on the top surface of the panel. They had better be marked in across the grain of the wood, not with it. The central line *c* should be cut down vertically about one-eighth of an inch with a chisel, starting each new cut from the previous one, and as the student is working across the grain, it will be as well to use the mallet (p. 64). For lines 1 and 2 the mallet will not be needed. Place the cutting edge of the chisel nearly parallel to *c*, and take a series of slanting cuts on either side, until *c* is reached.

Another way is to insert the corner of the chisel at the requisite slant, and push it along with the thumb of the left hand, spreading out the other fingers on the wood so as to get a firm grip. This sweeping cut is difficult, but it is excellent practice, and when dexterity is obtained, is often useful in cutting an outline, as one tool can then be made to do the work of three or four. Carvers' opinions differ as to the use of it.

In setting out fine V lines it is only necessary to pencil the centre line. It is more difficult to cut them with the grain of the wood, greater control of the tool being then required.

We will now consider the sampler of patterns (see illustration opposite). It has been derived from Italian, French, and English examples.

The first thing the student must do is to compare in column B, 8, 9, with 6 and 3, or 4, C, with 9, A. The effect of Nos. 8, 9, and 4, B, is poor in comparison with Nos. 6, 3, B, and 9, A, and yet they are all cut exactly in the same way, and take about the same time to do. These patterns are produced by two cuts of a gouge, variety being obtained by the length of the second cut and the way it is set out. In No. 8, B, the second cut is very short; in 6, B, it is rather longer; and in 3, B, considerably longer.

For the first cut insert the gouge almost vertically, inclining it at the cutting edge slightly outwards; if the wood be undercut it crumbles away. The second cut must slant exactly into the first cut; if it be taken deeper, the wood does not come out sharp and clean.

It is true that sometimes one has to go over the cuts again, but this should not be necessary if they be small. The aim of the student should be to make as few cuts as possible, the size depending on the tool used.

Compare 6, B, with a single line of 3, B, and 10, B, with 3, B. The latter is divided by a V line into three bands, and the effect is richer than at 10. Another combination at 7 shows the cuts continuous.

In French work the gouge-cut bands are usually defined by a V line on either side, but more frequently in England the V line is omitted, as at 6, with considerable loss of effect. When two or more rows are used, as at 10, B, the cuts alternate, up and down,

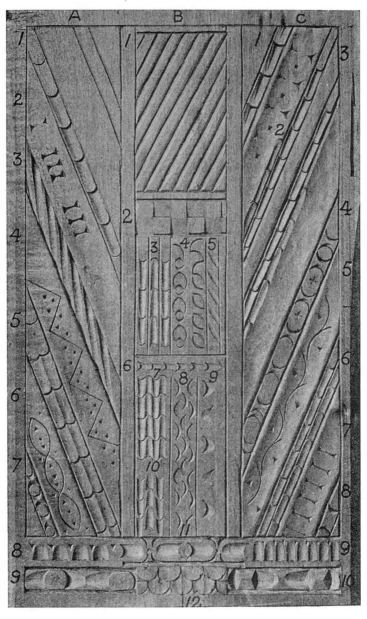

Sampler of Patterns.

Further varieties of the same cut may be seen at 1, 5, and 7, A, 1, 3, 4, 6, and 8, C. These gouge-cut patterns were a very marked feature of French work in the latter part of the fifteenth century, and were continued well on into the sixteenth century. They were also prevalent in England, examples being found on some of the bench-ends of the fifteenth century in the south-western counties, and on the chests, chairs, and various articles of furniture during the sixteenth and seventeenth centuries.

The flutes at 8, A, and 9, C (p. 43), cannot be done in two cuts. A flute requires to be of a uniform width, so that the second cut has to be widened and deepened at the top by further cuts. The base of the flute is cut with a chisel, and the second cut with a gouge, which is run into the chisel cut.

The flutes at 8, A, and 9, C, are separated at the top by a small triangular pocket, called by the chip-carver a sunk pocket, and is frequently to be met with in Gothic tracery.

The inner lines of the pockets are all cut from the centre outwards, pressing rather more heavily on the tool at the centre than on the outside. Where the lines are straight a chisel should be used, and a slightly curved tool, where the lines require it, as in the borders, C, 7 and 2. The wood is then sloped away from the edge to the centre. The triangles in the sampler at C, 2 and 7 (p. 43), have been done in this way, but at A, 2, and C, 5, they have been put in with a punch.

The flutes and reeded flutes (p. 26) were much used in England during the seventeenth century, and are very characteristic of the Jacobean style, but they were introduced at the end of Elizabeth's reign. In the examples at p. 43, 9, A, and 10, C, the surface of the wood has been slightly rounded over, and this further enhances the effect of the ornament. Most of these patterns look well on a bead moulding, or on a reeded surface (see chest, p. 26 and p. 49).

The triangular pockets at C, 7 (p. 43), are connected by a fine line, the outer sides being slightly curved.

Sometimes, as at Christchurch, in Hampshire, there is only a dot between the pockets instead of the incised line. It was towards the end of the fifteenth century in France that these cuts, like C, 7, came to be used, and they are a very marked feature on the bands, scrolls, ribbons, &c., of the early Renascence ornament in all countries. The same ornamentation may be seen on some linenfold panels in the Victoria and Albert Museum (No. 539-1892) removed from a house at Taunton, and dated late fifteenth century. It is probably a little later than that.

The scale pattern at 12, B (p. 43), is set out by a series of horizontal and vertical lines, the points of intersection X being the centres from which the semicircles are described. The scale is cut round vertically with a large gouge not quite so large as the semicircle, the tool being twisted round to complete the curve. The wood is then shaved away from the scale underneath, leaving a slight ridge in the centre, or it may be kept flat as in the figure on p. 63. Sometimes the scales are nicked on either side with a small veiner like the last three on sampler.

These *imbricated* patterns are very useful to the carver, and can be used on the scrolls of a cartouche, on a boss, as in the illustration on p. 63, for pilasters, and in a variety of ways (pp. 31-37). Elaborated examples are to be found on Italian and French furniture.

The other patterns on the sampler are too difficult

for the beginner to attempt, but they are described here
so as to keep the matter together.

Columns A and C of sampler (p. 43) consist of a series
of narrow and wide bands set out obliquely. The first
thing to do is to mark out these bands with a narrow V
groove, either with a V tool or a chisel. The narrow
bands are flat and ornamented with cuts previously
described, the wider bands are moulded. From each
side of the wider band a small chamfer is taken off, and
then a slight hollow is made between the chamfered
edges with a large flat gouge. The angle between hollow
and chamfer is then rounded off with a small tool, and
the moulded band ornamented.

The fine lines incised on 4 and 6, A, and 5, C (p. 43),
are very troublesome to do, but they are done on the
same principle as the V line described on p. 41, but
only a very small shaving of wood is taken out. Curved
tools must be used for 6, A, and 5, C. At C, 3 (p. 43),
it will be noticed that the outer row of gouge cuts are
carved on the edge of the moulded band, whereas at 6
the two rows are worked on the narrower flat band.
The gouge cuts at C, 3, are divided by a plain band
slightly rounded over, as at B, 1.

This pattern, B, 1, consists of a series of oblique lines,
run with a small veiner, the edges of which are chamfered
and then rounded over. It is a suitable decoration for
a small column, as in the French coffer.

The most difficult of all the patterns given in the
sampler is the twist or cable (A, 3). The band on which
it is carved must first be rounded over, and then the
lines, which should be long and oblique, pencilled in.
One line in the centre of each narrow flat band is sufficient. Between these lines the hollows are run with
a small gouge. Where the hollow dies off underneath,
it should be deepened rather more on one side than

the other. This helps to give the twisted effect which is required.

On the semicircular arches of the French chest (see

FRONT OF A FRENCH COFFER.

First half of Sixteenth Century. Victoria and Albert Museum, No. 312-1897.

illustration) the same cable appears, as well as on one of the ornamental bands in the linenfold pattern. This

chest is a very fine example of gouge-cut work. It has
formed the basis of the sampler, and should be studied
by all those interested in pattern work.

The only coarse work to be found in it are the three
leaves in the spandrels between the arches, and they are
considerably out of scale for the rest of the carving.

The front side only of the chest remains, and this
consists of five arches supported on columns, decorated
with alternating ornamental bands, different patterns
being on each column. Under each arch is a linenfold
panel, or as the French call it, " parchemin plié." It has
evidently been worked with the tools and not by the
joiner's plane, which was the common method of doing

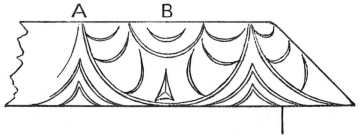

Enrichment of the Moulding on Lid of French Chest (p. 26).

it. The arches above the panel would stop the working
of the plane, so that in this case the carver's tools were
a necessity, as it is worked out of one piece of wood,
which is just over 1 in. thick.

The dimensions are as follows :—

Margin, $1\frac{3}{4}$ in.
Width of arch, $9\frac{3}{4}$ in.
Height and width of linenfold pattern, $19\frac{5}{8}$ in. by $5\frac{5}{8}$ in.
       ,,   ,,   capital, 3 in. by 2 in., necking, $2\frac{5}{8}$ in.
       ,,   ,,   base, $2\frac{3}{8}$ in.
       ,,   ,,   shaft of column, 12 in. by $2\frac{1}{2}$ in.
Total height of column, $17\frac{3}{8}$ in.

The French chest illustrated on p. 26 has various gouge-cut patterns on it ; the moulding to lid being treated as on p. 48. The gouge cuts might be a little deeper and the crescent shapes a little wider as they reach the outer semicircle. The semicircles should be cut with a smallish flat tool, which should be dragged round to follow the curve, and then a small shave of wood should be taken off from the other side. In the middle is a sunk pocket. Two of the carved mouldings from the front of the same chest are given in the annexed figure, A and C. The larger moulding on the outside of the stiles and muntins is carved like C—the inner carved moulding next to it like A, which is a double row of gouge cuts reversed. The small circular centre at C may be done with a blunt punch, or the end of an embossing tool for metal or leather will give the effect desired.

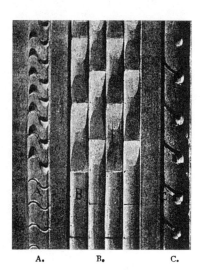

A.   B.   C.

A and C, from French Chest, No. 1,480.
B from some old Panelling at Rye,
Seventeenth Century.

On either side of the circular punch an oblique gouge cut is made, the cut being reversed on the outer and the inner edge. The section of the moulding is a quarter round (see p. 69). B in the figure above is copied from a piece of old panelling at Rye. The surface of the wood is first reeded and then the slanting cuts are made with a small flat. This pattern should only be used when the wood is thick, as it cuts deeper into the surface than the gouge-cut patterns. It is also more difficult to do.

The decoration of the beautiful Italian bowl (see figure) is purely the outcome of the tool. In any other material the ornamentation would be quite unsuitable.

WOODEN BOWL (ITALIAN).

Height, 4⅞ in. ; diameter, 6⅛ in.   Victoria and Albert Museum, No. 672-1891.

The treatment is very simple, merely the V line, the gouge cut, and the flute. The shape of the bowl is extremely graceful, and the ornament in no way detracts from its form, on the contrary it emphasises it. The horizontal bands are just where they should be, and the alternating bands at right angles to them are admirably proportioned. If a lid were added it would make a nice

tea caddy. The bowl came from Perugia, is probably
sixteenth-century work, but it is difficult to fix the date.
If the student is on the look-out for these simple

Panels from an Old Chest, Prestbury.

gouge-cut enrichments, he will be surprised to see how
often they recur. He will also find it exceedingly
interesting to evolve some patterns for himself, by
varying the combination of the cuts. Suggestions for
other simple carving are given in my small text-book
entitled " Chip Carving and other Surface Carving" (B. T
Batsford Ltd. In paper covers, price 1s. 6d. net, or bound
in cloth, lettered, 2s. net. Inland postage, 3d. extra).

Fourteenth-Century Miserere, Wells.

Top rail from an oak settle at Retford, English.   Date, 1704.

CHAPTER V

FLAT CARVING IN LOW RELIEF

WOOD-CARVING may be divided into three groups :—

First, Low Relief Carving, not exceeding a quarter of an inch projection from the ground.

Second, High Relief Carving, in which the projection varies considerably.

Third, Carving in the Round.

These three groups are dealt with in the subsequent chapters, the simplest work being taken first.   The student, however, in beginning his studies, is advised not to take them in the order given, but to start with the lessons in Chapter VIII.   After many years' experience I am convinced that high relief work affords the best practice, as it gives the student greater confidence and greater freedom.

The simplest style of carving (one frequently met with in Germany, Switzerland, and the Tyrol) is that in which only the ground is taken out, leaving the pattern perfectly flat, and not modelled at all (see figure opposite).   Unfortunately this style of work gives no scope to the carver, so that unless he can make his own designs he soon tires of it.

I will here explain how the pattern is marked out on the wood.   Set out the size of the wood on paper, and rule a vertical and horizontal line crossing one another exactly in the centre of the space set out.   Then draw in your pattern.   When completed make a tracing and be careful to emphasise the two central lines, but omit the boundary lines in the tracing.

Centre the panel in the same way as you did the drawing, and superimpose the lines of the tracing to those set out on the wood, so that they exactly correspond. Fix the tracing paper with drawing pins, taking care to place the pins only on those parts of the panel that are to be cut away. If they were placed on any surface not to be cut away, their marks would be visible,

Overdoor, from a late Fifteenth-Century Gothic Tyrolean Design.

to the disfigurement of the work. Having fixed the tracing paper with two pins, slip underneath the black or blue carbon transfer paper and secure it firmly with other pins. It is better to trace the pattern on to the wood and put the marginal lines in last, in case of any slight inaccuracy in the size of the panel. Trace the outline with a finely pointed H pencil, using a straight-edge and set square when the lines are straight and rectangular, and a compass for the circles or parts of circles. For these it is only necessary to mark through the tracing the centre of the circles and the radius, and then strike the lines direct on the wood with the compass. Instructions for grounding out are given in the next chapter. Most of this flat carving is executed in soft wood, and is rarely more than $\frac{1}{8}$ in. in relief, and often less. The sides of the pattern are slightly set out, and no attempt is made to make a flat and even background, which is small in area compared with the ornament which covers most of the surface. The turning over of the leaves and the interlacing of the stems and branches are merely suggested by lines cut with a V tool, and these lines should be strongly emphasised.

PANEL.

From a late Fifteenth-Century Gothic Church Bench. In the National Museum, Munich.

In the overdoor (p. 53), which was recently carved from an old Tyrolean design, the lines are weak, and are not as forcible as in the other examples. The carver also erred in isolating the pattern from the margin. This is rarely, if ever, to be found in the old work (see figures above and opposite), and is one of the reasons why it never looks as if the ornament had been fret cut and applied. The letters R.M.H. are cunningly introduced amongst the scrolls and foliage of the overdoor, and the general spacing out of the design is good. It must be remembered that in dealing with large surfaces, it is the broad effects that have to be considered.

Two panels from a German fifteenth-century church bench are given on this and preceding page. The carved

portion of the panel occupies two-thirds of it, and the lower part is left plain, a sensible arrangement, as the carving is placed where it is best seen. The relief is under $\frac{1}{8}$ in., and the ground spaces are small and left fresh from the cut of the tool. This gives a gradation of tone which could not otherwise be obtained. Portions of colouring remain, suggestive of old Flemish tapestry, and much more harmoni- ous than the colour one commonly meets

PANEL.

From a late Fifteenth-Century Gothic Church Bench. In the National Museum, Munich.

with. In this flat carving colour was largely used, both on the background and on the ornament, but modern restorations have been so garish and unsuccessful that one is driven to think that it is safest to let the wood alone. For interior work a judicious use of stains might be experimented with, but for out-of-door work oil paint would have to be used, and that is never very satisfactory, as by it the texture of the wood is lost.

A portion of the upper part of a large cupboard is given in the figure below. The battlemented top, being characteristic of the period, is carved with birds, treated in a simple, decorative way. The leaf and stick ornament, under the battlement, is also frequently to be met with at this date. The design of the frieze is graceful

GERMAN PANEL.

Late Fifteenth-Century Gothic.   In the National Museum, Munich.

in line, and the detail is slightly varied. The undersides of the leaves in the central scroll are cross-hatched with a V tool, and look remarkably well.

The geometric circles in the frieze do not amalgamate well with the rest of the design, and are pierced and planted on.

On the opposite page is a German chest of the latter part of the fifteenth century. It is carved in pine, and shows traces of having been coloured. The construction

PINE COFFER.

Late Fifteenth-Century Gothic. National Museum, Munich.

is somewhat rude, the upper rail being omitted. The lid has clamps of wood on either end like that on p. 24. The base has evidently been damaged, and the two blocks of wood on which it stands are a later addition. The *cusped* corners within these blocks are unnecessary and weak. The design of the ornament is admirable.

Another specimen of flat carving, but in quite a different style, is given on the opposite page, the front of an Italian chest.

The designs we have been considering have been the last phase of the Gothic style, although in the German chest (p. 57), in the distribution of the lines, the coming Renascence style is beginning to be felt.

The Italian chest could not be classified with either of these styles, in fact it would be difficult to classify it with any special style. The design and treatment is Oriental in feeling, and this influence is observable in a great deal of the carving of Northern Italy. The ornament is flat and in low relief, and the ground is punched with a very small triangular punch. The veins of the leaves are marked with a single line of punched dots, and the centre of the branches is defined in like manner.

In the other examples illustrated a V tool or veiner was employed, but these tools were never used by Oriental carvers, whose supply of tools was very limited.

By an intelligent use of the tool and the punch, in the chest opposite, the feathers of the birds have been successfully indicated, and completely differentiated from the equally successful fur in the animals. This chest, for simple, decorative carving, is both in treatment and design about as good as it could be.

Elaborate designs like those given from Germany and Italy are not to be met with in France and England.

FRONT OF A CHEST.

Northern Italy.   Fourteenth Century.   Width, 29 in. ; height, 17 in.   Berlin.

Part of Pilaster in the Oak Panelled Room from the "Old Palace" at
Bromley-by-Bow, which was built in 1605. English. Victoria
and Albert Museum, No. 248-1894.

In France the flat carving was usually confined to strapwork, where this class of work reached its highest perfection.

A great deal of flat carving was done in England during the Jacobean period, and an interesting example is given from the "Old Palace" at Bromley-by-Bow. It is a stepping stone for the carver from this chapter to the next, as the pattern is very slightly modelled. It is well designed, and the margin is skilfully worked in with the pattern, which is also well balanced with the ground spaces. The same may be noted in the examples from the staircase at Charterhouse, which was re-decorated by the Duke of Norfolk in 1565 for his contemplated marriage with Mary, Queen of Scots.

Charterhouse is a fine specimen of domestic architecture, and is of various dates. It contains some interesting carved woodwork, and is close to Aldersgate Street station.

Simple carved work has not been encouraged in England, and the opportunity has now come when we might develop a school for furniture, simply constructed, and simply carved, each student being taught to design, construct, and carve, on the lines suggested in this book.

Charterhouse Pilaster.

Frieze from a cabinet, French. Sixteenth century.

CHAPTER VI

STRAPWORK—MODELLING IN LOW RELIEF

THE student is advised as an elementary lesson to set
out a simple strapwork panel (see figure opposite),
rather larger than illustration, say 9 in. by 6¼ by ¾ in.,
on a panel of yellow pine.

The thickness of the wood is immaterial, as if thinner
wood were to hand, ⅜ in. would be sufficient. Pine, if
cut too thin, very soon twists (p. 18, l. 26).

Having traced the pattern on the wood, as described
on p. 52, the first thing to do is to remove the ground.
There are various ways of doing this. For rough work
in low relief, where the lines are broad and simple, the
outline may be cut down vertically with a tool. The
lines across the grain should always be cut first, otherwise the wood is liable to split. Use a mallet and
chisel for these, and for the curved lines an "extra
flat" (p. 64). Care should be taken not to undercut the pattern, the sides of which should be quite
vertical. It is better to err in setting the tool out, rather
than to set it in. Having cut the outline, remove the
wood from the centre with a small gouge, as shown in
the compartment at A. When the bulk of the wood has
been taken away, finish off the background with an
"extra flat," and if necessary use a small bent background tool for the angles. A shows the work in progress, whilst the similar compartments in the example
are completed. In the compartment at B a slightly

Strapwork Panel.   E. R.

1. Cutting the Lines across the Grain with a Chisel.

2. Cutting the Curved Lines with an " Extra Flat."

different method has been employed, although the difference is hardly apparent in the illustration.

Instead of cutting the outline it has been defined with a veiner (see figure). The tool must be held very firmly by both hands, and the handle of the tool kept low. The right hand pushes it forward, whilst the left hand guides it. The wrists must be free and lissom,

Outlining the Pattern with a Veiner.

and the carver should train himself to use either hand as required. After veining the outline, the wood is removed in the same way as at A, p. 63. Hardly any setting down is required in p. 63, as the relief is so slight, but the outline has to be touched up with the veiner as the process of removing the ground proceeds. At the sharp point above the letter B, the ground should be almost entirely removed from the side running with the grain before removing it from the side across the grain, when

Panel from a Sixteenth-Century French
Door.   Belfast Museum.

the wood should be cut away from the point where the wood is weak to where it is stronger.

For all low relief work and for lettering, the method of removing the ground as described at B is far better than that at A. If parts of the ornament require further detaching from the ground, the sides can always be set in as shown in section, p. 85.

In p. 63 the outer line of the pattern has been V grooved, and between this line and the edge of the panel the surface of the wood has not been touched. Within the outer band the ground

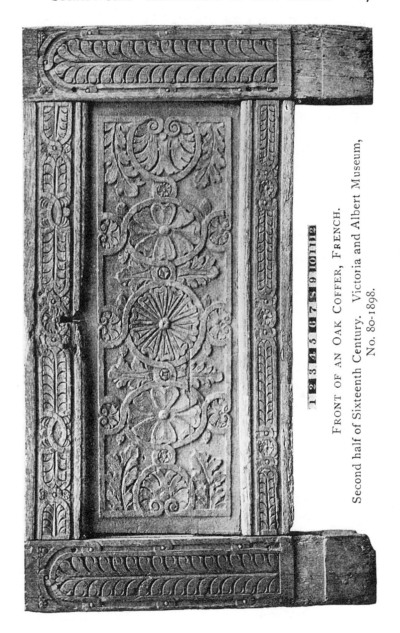

FRONT OF AN OAK COFFER, FRENCH.
Second half of Sixteenth Century. Victoria and Albert Museum,
No. 80-1898.

has been removed to a little under ⅛ in. The work must be done systematically, and all the ground should

be removed before starting on the ornament, with a few exceptions noted in Chapter VII. The next step is to *bost* in the ornament, and model it to the same stage throughout before finishing off any detail. The beads should then be cut with a gouge and rounded over, and the bands interlaced, the flatness of their surface being removed by a slightly curved gouge. The outline of the boss in the centre must be cut to the depth of ⅛ in., and then the wood should be rounded over and the scales drawn in. These should be kept flat, so as to preserve the contour, p. 45. The little shells are separated from the straps by a V groove, and then hollowed out as in the one at the top, the gouge cuts being put in at the last, as in the finished one at the bottom. If the outline were fret cut

FRENCH STRAPWORK DOOR.

Sixteenth Century. Glasgow Museum.
Height, 13½ in. ; width, 15 in.

of this small panel, it could be utilised for the ends of a book rack, but at least 1 in. of wood beyond the outline at the bottom should be left to give stability to the base.

A similar but more elaborate example is the panel from a sixteenth-century French door (p. 66). To complete the panel, the upper part of the pattern would have to be repeated below.

The *guilloche* ornament between the oval bosses adds richness to the effect.

The French coffer (p. 67) is coarser in execution, but more varied in design. The way it could be utilised is given at p. 23. If the student has mastered the instructions previously given, he would find no difficulty in carving this. The centre panel is a repeating pattern, and could be adapted to various sizes.

The illustrations on this and the preceding

FRENCH STRAPWORK DOOR.

Sixteenth Century. Glasgow Museum.
Height, 12½ in. ; width, 5¾ in.

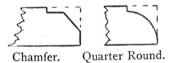

Chamfer.   Quarter Round.

page are from two very pretty French strapwork doors in the Glasgow Museum. In the original doors the panel is duplicated, and a plain muntin forms the central division. Simple as they look a beginner would not find them as easy to do as either

PANEL FROM A CUPBOARD, FRENCH (LYONS).

Forming the Base of a Chair of State, of Carved Walnut.   Second
half of Sixteenth Century.   F. Pierpont Morgan Coll.

of the examples on pp. 63 or 67. There is greater variety in the lines, and the ground spaces are smaller, so that it requires considerable control of the tool to keep the bands to the proper width, with their correct interlacements. The small pateræ and rosettes on p. 69 have first been grounded out in a complete circle, and the modelling started for the centre one, as per section on

Mouldings which Frame in the Panel opposite.

p. 85. The divisions were then drawn in, and the wood removed from the spaces between with a small grounder.

It is always more satisfactory in a rosette to have an odd number of divisions, as in the panel on p. 69, than an even number, as in that on p. 68.

The small moulding round the centre circle of the panel on p. 68 has first been lowered about $\frac{1}{16}$ in. below the bands, the outer angle has then been chamfered off afterwards and rounded over, and the pattern has then

Panel from a Sixteenth-Century
French Door.

been drawn in (p. 69.2). It consists of a simplified egg and tongue, which is merely indicated by the cuts of a gouge.

We have a still more elaborate example (p. 70), the treatment of which requires considerable experience and skill. It forms the lower panel of a chair of state, and is less than $\frac{1}{8}$ in. in relief. In addition to the strapwork, there are some floriated scrolls which are very delicately modelled. Note in these the little hollow that runs round the inner curve ; this is the most difficult thing to execute in the whole design. The same feature is seen in the very charming sixteenth-century French stool (p. 29).

The panel looks infinitely better when seen with the mouldings that frame it in (p. 71), as they protect the

carving, a point not to be overlooked. The edge of
the panel is finished off with a small ogee moulding,
and then there is a chamfer before the inner ogee
moulding is reached. The mouldings are given to
the same scale as the panel. The *guilloche*, the interlacing strapwork moulding, is delicately carved, and is
frequently used with French strapwork, but the leaf
moulding is coarsely treated, and the bead and astragal
come too close upon it.

The panel on p. 72 is another fine example of French
strapwork, which for beauty of design and delicacy of
treatment cannot be surpassed. A cast from the original
is in the Victoria and Albert Museum, No. 1893-496.

Further details from the Staircase, Charterhouse.   Date, 1565.

It is a good plan to note any lines and features in
the old work that are pleasant, and then to try and
combine them in a fresh design. When this is done, the
original *motif* is often hardly traceable, yet it formed
the basis on which to build up.

Detail from top rail of a Coffer, French.   Sixteenth century.

CHAPTER VII

LOW RELIEF WORK (CONTINUED)

THE width of the margin in relation to the panel, as well as the treatment of the margin, are important points for the carver to consider when the panel is not rebated, but is prepared and let into the framework, as Fig. 3, p. 21 (I.).

When the carving is framed it is not necessary to have as wide a margin as when it is not framed, as the sides and lid of a box, the sides of a pilaster, &c.

The position of the object also affects the width of the margin, as when there is a projection over the carving the width of the margin has to be slightly increased.

If the lid projects over the sides of the box, the upper margin should be a little wider than the others.

If the margin comes considerably below the eye the surface is foreshortened, and an allowance should be made for this.

The amateur carver in his zeal invariably over-decorates the surface of the wood, and does not realise the importance of a plain surface as a means of giving value to the carving.

With regard to the treatment of the margin, it may be set down straight when the design is in low relief and touches the margin, as in the Exeter example (p. 81), or as in the chair back panel (p. 77), or the pedestal of pilaster (p. 83), where the margin forms part of the design, or in strapwork panels (p. 68), on account of

74

the rectangular edges of the bands. Generally speaking, for low relief work it is better to use a gouge than a chisel, and slope the sides of the margin into the ground. If this treatment does not suit the design, an allowance should be made in the margin for a small hollow to be run on each side with a gouge. In preparing for the hollow the wood should first be wasted away into the ground with a gouge. The sides of the margin should then be set down with a chisel, and finished off with a veiner when the ground is cleared up. The width

End of a Box, Oak. Date about 1660.

of the hollow having been marked in with a hard pencil, the four corners should then be cut mitrally with a chisel and the sides chamfered into these cuts. The hollow should then be run along the chamfers with a gouge, being careful to make the cuts meet properly at the mitre.

A simple but effective Jacobean pattern is given in the above figure. It is the end of a box, and the curve of the oval has suffered slightly in being compressed into a fixed space. These oval medallions are very common in seventeenth-century work, and are treated in various ways. Sometimes the medallions are reversed, and are carved with an alternating pattern. Sometimes the inner surface is slightly moulded and decorated with gouge cuts like the shells on the pedestal. In the box end the ground is judiciously blended with the pattern, and is an example in which the ground should be removed as much as possible with a small fluter, and only the lobes of the leaves, the small channels in the centre, and the eye of the volutes should be set down. In utilising this pattern for a morticed and tenoned frame the student must find out how much wood there is above the surface of the joints, and treat the pattern accordingly. It would be as well to convert the oval into a circle at the corners, as the rails would centre better with the circle than the oval. The pattern would not adapt well for a mitred joint.

The back of a chair or settle is not a suitable place to display the skill of the carver, and on examining good old examples we shall find for these articles of furniture the carving was flat and in very low relief. A very good example of a seventeenth-century chair is given on p. 77. The construction is strong and simple, and the carving is not elaborate. The free cut ornament at the top is graceful in outline and very effective, though so simply carved. This is in a large measure due to the pattern not being grounded out. The stiles being carried above the rail and rounded over at the top, adds much to the charm of the design. The way they are carved is a very noticeable feature in the furniture of the sixteenth century in France. Compare them with the French chest (p. 67) in which the surface of the stiles is kept flat and not moulded.

The stiles of the chair are moulded like the section of the leaf (p. 85), except that the original surface of the wood is left up at the edges. On the direction of

ARM CHAIR, OAK.   Date about 1620.

77

the gouge cuts much of the grace of line depends, and
for this the French work is usually better than the
English.   The stiles of the chair present a smooth
surface, and there is nothing to catch or to break off.

The *guilloche* band on the top rail is very well carved,
but the circles at either end should have been completed.
This would have given a better joint, and the rail would
not look, as it does now, as if it had been cut off from a
longer length.   The lower rail has the same fault.   It
has two carved mouldings which are ornamented with
gouge-cut patterns.

The centre panel is $\frac{1}{8}$ in. in relief, and is carved with
one of the popular designs of the seventeenth century,
the interlacing circles.   When set out on a square the
space between the circles is omitted.   In the chair panel
leaves with parallel veined lines are put in to increase
the width.   These lines are not at all easy to do, or are
the moulded bands of the circles.   The method of working was described at p. 46.   The rest of the carving
presents no difficulty.   The rosette in the centre of the
panel and the one above might be improved by substituting for the punched radiating lines V grooves, and by
ornamenting the divisions with gouge cuts, in the manner
suggested in Chapter IV. and in the French coffer
illustrated on p. 67.

It is important that the treatment should be kept
flat, so as to cause no friction when in use, especially in
the centre of the back.   A point the modern carver is
especially asked to note.

The gouge-cut patterns on the mouldings of the
lower rail are very effective and most suitable for the
decoration of domestic furniture, either on flat or
moulded surfaces.

In the old work the panels were often not grounded
out, the outline of the design being simply marked in

PANEL OF THE DOOR OF A WALL CUPBOARD, SYRIAN.

Late Eighteenth Century.   Height, 14⅝ in. ; width, 10¾ in.
Victoria and Albert Museum, No. 900-1884.

with a deep V groove. The pattern was then slightly
modelled or merely ornamented with tool cuts. The

designs of the Prestbury panels (p. 51) could be treated in either of these ways.

Elizabethan and Jacobean carving furnishes plenty of examples for simple work, but they are so well known that it has not been thought necessary to give further illustrations here.

A very interesting example of simple work is the door from Syria (see p. 79), although the expert wood-carver would probably view it with contempt. The object of the craftsman was no doubt to produce a pleasing decorative effect with the minimum amount of work, and in this he has certainly succeeded.

The example should not be copied literally, but the student should study it and vary it as his fancy may suggest.

The very free way in which the carving is executed would be entirely lost if a slavish reproduction were to be attempted. The circle above the base is chip-carving pure and simple, and in fact the whole of the carving is but slightly removed from the chip-carving treatment, which consists of short and direct cuts, in contradistinction to the long sweeping cuts used in more elaborate work.

The chip-carver would easily master the technical difficulties presented in the Syrian example, and he would find in it a fresh field for design, and a pleasing variety to the monotony of the work at present designated as " Chip-Carving."

The Egyptian lotus-flower and the Persian carnation are valuable *motifs* for this branch of carving.

The simple gouge-cut pattern (p. 43.10) of the vase is very effective. The ground of the carving is not uniformly flat, as it varies in depth from $\frac{1}{8}$ in. to $\frac{3}{1}$ in. The student would probably get the best effect by working the pattern and the ground together. A bent background

CARVED OAK PANEL.

Removed from an Old House near Exeter.   About 1600.   Sight Measure of Carving, 5 ft. 9 in. by 2 ft. 10 in.

Victoria and Albert Museum, Nos. 4870 to 4881-1856.

CARVED OAK PILASTER. About 1600. Sight Measure of Carving, 4 ft. 11 in. by 10 in.; Capital, 12 in. by 10 in. Removed from an Old House near Exeter. Victoria and Albert Museum, Nos. 4870 to 4881-1856.

tool would not be necessary, but a V or small veiner would be useful for some of the angles.

Three illustrations are given from a panelled room removed from an old house near Exeter, and for broad, simple Renascence carving no better examples could be found. The panelling was probably imported from Flanders, as there are several similar rooms in and about Exeter, all of which give evidence of having been adapted to the rooms in which they have been fitted.

The carving of the panelling does not exceed $\frac{1}{8}$ in. in relief, and where greater relief was wanted, as in the boss of the pedestal, the wood has been planted on. This is an expedient which is rarely to be commended. The panel on p. 81 and the pilaster would be very good for the student to copy, as the modelling is simple, and the treatment can easily be seen in the illustrations. In the panel, if the pendant centre were omitted, the student would have the typical Tudor rose of the period.

The treatment of the vine in the pilaster is excellent, and the tendrils are but slightly undercut. The stalk and branches might be a little less round. Notice that the upper margin is wide, as it is well above the eye and under a projecting moulding, and that the margin of the base which rests upon the pedestal is a little narrower, but slightly wider than the sides. When seen *in situ* these differences are not apparent.

The boss in the centre of the pedestal has been applied. The treatment of the shell-like ornaments is very simple and most effective. They appear again in the four corners of a square panel, with a cherub's head in the centre of the panel, the wood for which has also been planted on.

The capital is a very typical example of the style, and comparatively easy to carve. The width at the base of the capital should always be the same as the width of the pilaster.

PEDESTAL OF PILASTER.
Sight Measure of Carving,
3 ft. 6½ in. by 15 in.

Of the examples given in this chapter the Venetian box (p. 84), for a beginner, would be the most difficult to execute on account of the size, but for anyone who had any facility with his tools the carving would be quite simple.

Eight small holes may be noticed in the cover
where the spiral reverses, and these were once filled in
with precious stones. If the jewels were omitted the

COVER OF BOX, VENETIAN.

Second half of Fourteenth Century.   Height, 4½ in. ; diameter, 4 in.
Victoria and Albert Museum, No. 1153·64.

ground might be carved so as to be slightly raised at
these points, and a carved rosette substituted for the
metal centre. This would have to be allowed for in
the section prepared for the turner. The pattern and
the background should be worked together.

CHAPTER VIII

MODELLING IN HIGH RELIEF

THE remarks in the preceding chapters have been confined to quite simple carving, but there is no doubt that even to gain proficiency in this, some preliminary studies in high relief carving are a great advantage. To obtain freedom with the tools and wrist no better studies can be found than those in use at the School

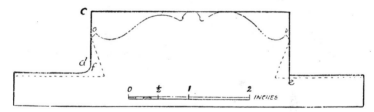

Section of Leaf on the Line AB.

of Art Wood Carving, South Kensington. They give a technical insight of the craft not otherwise obtainable.

I will therefore conclude this elementary treatise with the two first lessons usually given at the school.

LESSON I.—THE LEAF (p. 86).

Procure a piece of the best yellow pine, size of illustration and 1 in. thick, and glue it on to a board, but before securing the board to the bench a line should be gauged round the sides of the wood to the depth of

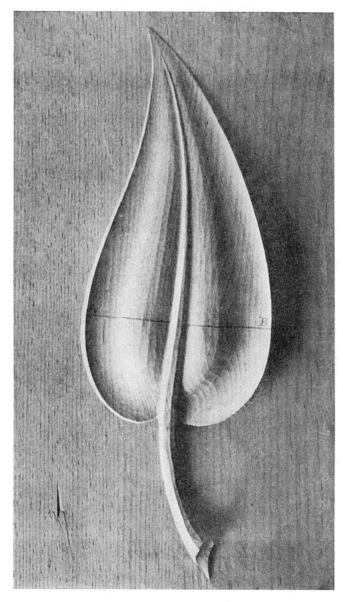

LEAF (I.).

the relief required, which is $\frac{5}{8}$ in. for the leaf.   From the outside edge of the panel, with a large gouge, cuts are run up to the outline of the leaf as shown in the demonstration No. I.   The corner of the tool must be kept free, *i.e.*, above the surface of the wood.   If once the tool becomes embedded in it, it is likely to get broken and the wood to split.   As the tool reaches

Removing the Wood from the Background.

the outline it requires to be brought gradually to the surface.

Do as much work with one tool as you can.   A quick gouge can be utilised in many ways by using only part of the curve, and pressing lightly upon it if a flatter cut is required.   To change the tools unnecessarily is a great loss of time.

Having removed the wood roughly from the ground in the manner described, the outline of the leaf should be cut round vertically with tools that fit the curve, and

the ground made even with an "extra flat." Study the
section on the line AB.

At this stage keep the ground slightly higher than
the depth finally intended, the first line in section, and
finish it off to the dotted line after the leaf is modelled
and undercut.

In cutting the outline of a pattern, the sides should

Modelling the Leaf.

be kept vertical. On no account should they be undercut until after the surface of the pattern is modelled, or
as the wood-carver calls it, *bosted in*. It is, however,
important that the vertical cuts should not go beyond
the level of the ground, as at *e*. To avoid this it is
better to stop the cuts a little above the required depth,
and then to use a veiner or small fluter, as at *f*. This
prevents the ground from being spoiled by preliminary
cuts. The outer lines of section show the wood pre-

pared previous to modelling. The inner line gives the contour on the line AB. The dotted lines show the position of the sides after they have been undercut and the level of the ground when finished. The ground being removed, the next thing to do is to get the shape of the leaf as seen in profile before modelling in the detail. This rule applies to all modelled work.

The highest part of the leaf is along the line AB, and from this cut away the wood to the tip. When the requisite incline has been obtained, loosen the screw and turn the block round, and slope the wood towards the stalk. The cuts along the stalk require a little humouring, as the wood is narrow, and therefore has not much resisting power. The tools can only be worked by straight and downward strokes, and cannot be forced up an incline.

After the undulation of the leaf is finished, the stem is marked in on either side with a small veiner. Then take a large gouge and model the curve at the side, as the carver is doing in demonstration II. The hollow or concave curve having been put in, the rounded or convex curve is obtained by rounding over the angle of the wood, where it meets the hollow, and on either side of the central stem, with an "extra flat" tool. The stem of the leaf has four surfaces, and this is much more effective than a rounded or single angle treatment. The sides of the stem should be finished off with a veiner, which is far better for this purpose than a V tool, which would make it too detached. When the modelling is completed, mark in a graceful outline with a soft pencil and chamfer the edge up to this line, then undercut the sides, leaving a bevelled edge as in section. The tip of the leaf should not be undercut, as in parts the outline should die off into the ground.

FIVE-LOBED LEAF (II.).

LESSON II.—A FIVE-LOBED LEAF (p. 90).

The ground is removed in the same way as in the first lesson, except that the point at CD being weak a little extra wood must be left in the first stage. Cut the outline at C and then lower CD, which is about $\frac{1}{16}$ in. from the ground, before cutting the complete outline at D. After the thickness of the wood has been reduced, the outline at D can easily be marked in, and if cut, then the strain on the weak point is considerably lessened. The carver frequently has to have recourse to this practice, but the outline on one side must be secured, or else the leading lines may be lost.

Where the × is put the wood has been left the full height. Point A is $\frac{3}{8}$ in. in relief, B $\frac{1}{8}$ in. Having sloped the *lobes* and the stalk, draw in the central lines, and mark these in with a veiner or a V tool, being careful to note how they radiate from E. Avoid keeping the general effect at one level, undulation is required. This lesson is a curious study for the grain of the wood, as it will mostly be found in executing it in pine that if the wood on the right side of the central vein cuts downwards, C will have to be cut upwards, D downwards, and so alternately round the leaf. When *bosting in,* the grain of the wood must carefully be observed, and if it appear to splinter or tear stop cutting at once and begin from another direction.

When the modelled surface has been carefully finished off, bevel the edge and slightly undercut the sides.

The leaves of the Misereres, if enlarged, on pp. 19, 39, 51, would make excellent studies.

INDEX

*For definitions of words marked with an asterisk,
see Appendix on opposite page*

APPENDIX

Bosting in.—The term is used for the preliminary stages in modelling, and is taken from the French *ébaucher*, to sketch.

Clamp or **Cleat.**—A strip of wood, or iron, fastened on transversely to a board or a panel in order to give strength, to prevent warping, or to hold in position.

Cusp.—The projecting points of foils or foliations.

Foils.—The arcs on either side of the cusps.

Guiloche or **Guilloche.**—An ornament in the form of two or more interlacing bands, or straps, twisting over a series of knobs or eyes, at regular intervals, in a continued series of spirals, pp. 77, 78.

Imbricated.—Anything that lies one over the other, as the scales of a fish, the leaf buds of a plant, hops, &c., pp. 37-63.

Miserere.—The projecting bracket on the underside of the seats of stalls in mediæval churches and chapels.

Ogee—Ovolo.—An ogee is a moulding formed of a concave and a convex curve, and is "wave-like" in appearance. It is the same as the Cyma Recta, and the Cyma Reversa. Example, top member, below the fillet section, p. 34.

The ovolo is the same as the egg moulding, and is usually a quarter of a circle, p. 69. Second moulding on section, p. 34. In Jacobean and French work it is sometimes flatter, and carved with a variety of patterns suitable to the curve of the moulding. Third moulding on section. The first group of mouldings represents the cornice—the flat band is the frieze, and the group below is the architrave, the terms and grouping being based on classic architecture.

Rebate.—A plain square sinking on the edge of a board or panel, p. 21, 3 (II.), or a moulding, p. 22, l. 16.

Spandrel or **Spandril.**—The triangular space between the outer mouldings of two contiguous arches or circles, or parts of circles, with a horizontal moulding or band above them.

Head-piece to Chapter VIII. From Cannonbury House, Islington. Time of James I.

Note.—The student is advised to pay special attention to the designing of letters and numerals, so as to make them an integral part of the design and suitable in character to the style in which he is carving.

PRACTICAL
WOODCARVING
ELEMENTARY AND ADVANCED

CARVED DOOR, KING'S COLLEGE, CAMBRIDGE.
Date 1531-1535.

PRACTICAL WOODCARVING
ELEMENTARY AND ADVANCED

ELEANOR ROWE

PART II
ADVANCED WOOD-CARVING

DOVER PUBLICATIONS, INC.
MINEOLA, NEW YORK

CONTENTS

Thirteenth-Century Miserere in Exeter Cathedral.

INTRODUCTION

THE author has been encouraged by the way "Practical Wood-Carving" was received to publish a second edition, in two parts.

Part I. deals with simple carving, gradually advances to slightly modelled detail in very low relief, and ends with a chapter on high relief, which requires more modelling of the surface.

Part II., the present volume, gives examples of more advanced work, attempts to explain the method of carving, and suggests to the student points by which he may be enabled to note the characteristics of the different styles. It is designed for the student who is unable to procure personal instruction, but it is hoped that it will interest the practical wood-carver, the designer, and those who seek for general information on the subject.

Part II. has been carefully revised, and a great deal of matter added to the text, 11 new photographs added, as well as several new line drawings. It would have altered completely the plan of the book if the illustrations had been placed in chronological sequence, but a few suggestions are given in this chapter with regard to the periods touched upon in the pages that follow. A table with a summary of the different styles follows this Introduction. The classification of the Gothic style is taken from E. S. Prior's "Gothic Art in England," and for the Renascence period, Reginald Blomfield's "History of Renascence Architecture in England" is quoted.

On the left-hand side of the Gothic periods has been added the popular nomenclature, and the same will be found in the Renascence period in the centre column. The influence of the various styles upon carved woodwork can be touched upon only very briefly here. It forms but a small detail of a very vast subject that has its root in Architecture, and which, like a tree, throws forth its branches, great and small. The most reliable evidence as to the change of style is to be found in the mouldings, and these naturally affected the ornament with which they were enriched. It must be borne in mind that the evolution from one style to another was very gradual, and that there was usually a period of transition not infrequently of long duration. In some places the change took place much later than in others, so that there is often an overlapping of styles. Only a few examples can be given of the different periods, and one may be mentioned of the Norman transition time, a billet moulding on the wooden screen at old Shoreham Church.

The first division of the Gothic style, the "Early English," is not so diffuse in its ornament as the later styles, and is more easy to recognise than these. In Exeter Cathedral there is a unique series of misereres, dating from 1224-44. One is illustrated here as a typical example of the Early English three-lobed leaf. The student who is pursuing his archæological study only from ornament, will find the conventional leaf and its treatment an excellent starting-point for his investigations. Its shape and treatment differ in every style, and it is a characteristic feature of the ornament. Natural foliage was also used, but the gradual and subtle changes that took place in the treatment of this, the student must note for himself. The old thirteenth-century stalls in Salisbury Cathedral (p. 36) are the most complete examples of the Early English period ; not only the ornament but the typical capitals and mouldings of the style are there recorded. Two carved capitals are preserved at Peterborough Cathedral and two misereres at Christ Church, Hants, one of which with the dragon has a close resemblance to one at Exeter.

There is a thirteenth-century miserere in Henry VII.'s Chapel at Westminster, and other examples are to be found elsewhere. The three-lobed or trefoil leaf is the conventional and characteristic leaf of the period, but in the Exeter series some good carving is to be found of natural leaves, which may be compared with the early fourteenth-century misereres in Wells Cathedral, illustrated in Part I. The leaves of the former are less serrated, and the modelling of the surface is flatter than in the Decorated period. There are numerous grotesques, animals, &c., in the Exeter series, and two remarkably fine carved heads, which testify that the thirteenth-century English wood-carver had reached a very high standard. St Mary's Hospital, Chichester, has an interesting wooden screen, which may be cited as an example of the geometrical period ; it was executed about 1280. It shows in its construction how much the wood-worker was under the influence of the stone mason, and in the years that follow this is very evident in the ornament, as the student may see for himself, in comparing the Bishop's Throne with the Sedilia in Exeter Cathedral. Passing on to the Decorated period, the stalls in Winchester Cathedral should be studied. They are early examples of the period, full of dignity and grace, with their crocketed gables, geometrical tracery, and pierced panels of natural foliage, set slightly forward from the background. In Chichester Cathedral the fourteenth-century misereres are fine examples of the carver's skill of the non-conventional type. Illustrative of a more conventional treatment, the Bishop's Throne at Exeter is a first-rate example of the Decorated period in the first quarter of the fourteenth century. Space only permits the finial and a detail from one of the niches on p. 38 to be given, but it is sufficient to show the change on the previous style.

The Perpendicular style which followed extended over a long period. It was then that the wood-carver came more fully into his own, recognising that wood required a very different treatment from stone. Examples of this style abound everywhere, and several illustrations are given in the text from Devonshire. Richly carved crestings are a very noticeable feature. In the Norfolk churches, in addition to the screens, there are some fine canopies for the fonts, and numerous carved bosses on the wooden roofs.

The examples from Hexham (p. 34) should be noted, as the battlemented coping and segmental arch are very typical of the later period.

As time went on the foliage became thin and attenuated, and the drill largely took the place of the gouge. The same patterns were repeated over and over again ; the life, the vigour had passed away, and a dull mechanical makeshift was all that was left, a mere ghost of the past.

Under the subdivision of Tudor, we may class the

linenfold panel, for which the joiners and the carvers were together responsible. It made its appearance in England about the middle of the fifteenth century. At first the folds were simple, and if ornamented only with incised work. Later the folds increased, and all sorts of floral embellishments were introduced. The stalls in Henry VII.'s Chapel at Westminster are a fine example of the period, but they are not very typical of the style. Nevertheless they are well worthy of study. The decoration of the columns of the stalls is an interesting feature of the work, and the same treatment was very frequent in France towards the end of the fifteenth century. It is possible that the beautiful decorated columns to be found in the Romanesque work of Italy, both in the churches and the cloisters, may have had an influence on the wood-carver ; in any case the enrichment greatly adds to the decorative effect of the whole. The same may be noted in the woodwork of the Spring chantry at Lavenham.

In concluding the notes on the Gothic period, the student should compare the conventional leaves of the Exeter Miserere, the Bishop's Throne, Exeter, and the example from Hexham Abbey.

In the early English example the leaf is composed of a trefoil leaf, non-serrated in outline, probably based on the clover.

In the Decorated example of the finial, the vine leaf is used, and the boundary or mass line (p. xv) is composed of four straight lines. The leaf is bossy and very highly modelled, and seen in profile takes an ogee line.

In the Perpendicular period the leaf at Hexham Abbey is nearly square in outline, the elongation of the stalk being necessary for the crockets. The carving is flatter and still more conventionalised. In the example from Etchingham, Part I., it is quite square, and is very suggestive of the wood-carver's tools. As time went on the leaf was spaced out into a series of squares or diamonds, without any cohesion or growth, and all interest in the carving ceased.

The dawn of the sixteenth century saw the influence of the Italian workmen, or the beginning of the Renascence style in England. The Gothic traditions had practically died out, and a new style was welcomed that might give a fresh impetus to arts and crafts (p. 31, "Waltham Abbey" Panelling, Part I.). The years that followed may be divided into two periods (see Table, p. xvi). The Early Period includes the styles popularly, though not logically, called the Elizabethan and the Jacobean. The Later Period embraces the so-called Queen Anne, Georgian, and Adam styles.

No more beautiful example can be found in England of the early period, under Italian influence, than the panelling at King's College, Cambridge, illustrated in the frontispiece. The construction and proportion of the door, the fine carving of the pilasters, panels, emblems, and initials, and the heraldic treatment of the Royal Arms must excite our admiration. The design is eminently fitted for the material for which it is intended, and the "metallic" treatment, so noticeable in the woodwork of the later period, is entirely absent. The initials of Henry VIII. and Anne Boleyn fix the date from 1531-35. In one place the "Bluebeard" has added on J. S. (Jane Seymour), to whom he was married the day after he had caused "the sweet Anne" to be beheaded.

During the reign of Elizabeth, the foreign influence was mainly German, introducing as it did the pyramidal or nailhead decoration, terminal pilasters, rustication, strapwork, and bulbous detail, enriched with acanthus leaves or gadroons (p. 58); features absolutely foreign to Gothic art. Side by side with this exaggerated style lingered the Tudor traditions, and the Elizabethan mansion is full of charm. The simple furniture that adorned its interior carries with it some of the best traditions of the wood-worker, not only for its excellent construction, but the sound principles which governed the ornamentation. Towards the end of the sixteenth century the modified Classic cornice appears in the woodwork, with the dental band generally slightly enriched and the cyma carved with the acanthus or water leaf. It is impossible to draw a line of demarcation with the woodwork termed Elizabethan or Jacobean, as the latter style was in vogue before Elizabeth had died, but as time went on, the exaggerated details were modified, and the Italian influence, under Inigo Jones, began again to be felt in the buildings erected during the reign of Charles I. The woodwork continued for some time on the Jacobean lines, but during the seventeenth century many fine staircases were built, which, as the century advanced, developed a more Renascence character, culminating with Sir Christopher Wren, with whom Grinling Gibbons was so frequently associated.

The Queen Anne style, a subdivision of the later period, was the result of the Dutch influence, which William and Mary supported. It was not so ornate as the woodwork of the previous style, but the carving was simple and direct; every cut tells, and the foliage is massed rather than undulated. The carved mouldings round the chimney-pieces and doors were bold, whilst points of interest were centralised in the frieze of the fireplace and the pediment of the door or overmantel.

A school of excellent carvers continued through the first half of the eighteenth century, as is testified by several examples, removed from houses in or near

London, which may be seen in the Victoria and Albert Museum.

Towards the middle and until the end of the eighteenth century there was a constant change of style, concurrent with the Renascence work initiated by Inigo Jones and carried on by Sir Christopher Wren and other architects connected with him. Sir William Chambers continued to work in the Classic style, indulging at the same time in Chinese Art and gardening. Thomas Chippendale followed this up in his furniture workshop, where he also made the French Rococo style very popular. There was also an attempt at a Gothic revival, but although Chippendale tried to incorporate the detail, the furniture on those lines was not a success. He executed a great deal of very excellent furniture, but it is as a chair-maker that his name is known in every household. Few people associate with his name the florid, delicate carving of the gilded mirrors, girandoles, clock cases, etc., which were turned out in his workshop.

In the Georgian or second subdivision of the later period, the carved wooden chimney-piece gives way to that in marble, but the changes are too subtle to dwell upon in this short treatise.

Under the brothers Adam a much more refined style set in, mainly influenced by the careful measured drawings made by Robert Adam of the Emperor Diocletian's palace at Spalato. There was still scope for the carved capital, but the mouldings were sparsely and delicately carved, and the carving on the chairs was much restrained. Inlay took the place of carving, and the wood-carver's art lost its prestige, and the cabinet-maker's art was brought to perfection.

A number of carved objects illustrative of the historic styles may also be studied in the Victoria and Albert Museum, both English and foreign (and photographs of the majority are obtainable at the museum bookstall). There is a wide range of geometric subjects, but, in addition, the museum examples give a good selection for study of foliage and the way it is treated in almost all the periods under review.

The suggestions very briefly indicated in this chapter must be read in conjunction with the text and with the illustrations that follow.

Examples found in England are called English, as the vexed question as to foreign or English craftsmanship cannot be dealt with here.

Finial from the Bishop's Throne,
Exeter Cathedral. Fourteenth Century.

CLASSIFICATION OF ENGLISH STYLES FROM THE MIDDLE OF THE TWELFTH TO THE EARLY NINETEENTH CENTURY. (*Dates only approximate; included for general guidance.*)

GOTHIC.

EARLY ENGLISH {	1150 to 1200	Transition from Norman to Lancet.
	1200 to 1250	Lancet.
DECORATED - {	1250 to 1300	Geometrical.
	1300 to 1350	Curvilinear or Flowing.
PERPENDICULAR {	1350 to 1450	Perpendicular or Rectilinear.
	1450 to 1525	Tudor.

RENASCENCE.

THE EARLY PERIOD, 1500 to 1640.	1500 to 1550.	The influence of the imported Italian workmen during the reign of Henry VIII.
	Elizabethan, 1550 to 1600. Jacobean, 1600 to 1640.	The influence of the German and Flemish workmen who sought shelter in this country.
THE LATE PERIOD, 1640 to 1820.	Transitional, 1640 to 1660.	The influence of Inigo Jones (1573-1653).
	Late Stuart and Queen Anne, 1660 to 1720.	The influence of Wren (1648-1720). The influence of the French refugees who sought shelter here after the Revocation of the Edict of Nantes in 1683. The Dutch influence under William and Mary.
	Georgian, 1720 to 1760.	The influence of Sir William Chambers (1726-1796) and other Palladian Architects. Interludes of Rococo and Chinoiséne influence.
	Adam, 1760 to 1790.	The influence of the brothers Adam (Robert, 1728-1792). The influence of the later French styles.
	Regency, 1790 to 1820.	The Greek Revival, with later eclecticism.

PRACTICAL WOOD-CARVING

CHAPTER I

GOTHIC CARVING—TRACERY

THE use of the word tracery by modern writers is derived from Sir Christopher Wren, but in mediæval contracts the term does not appear.

It is taken by the wood-carver from the stone-carver, but the former must bear in mind that the conditions that regulate his work are very different to the latter.

In wood-carving the tracery has no definite weight to bear, and is used more or less ornamentally, so that the wood-carver can have a freer hand and a greater scope for his fancy. It has fallen

QUATREFOLIATED CIRCLE.
(English, Modern.)

Size of Wood, 9 in. square by ¾ in. thick.

into disrepute because the carver, instead of letting his imagination have free play, has coerced himself by geometrical rules, and has aimed at mechanical precision rather than balance of line and sweetness of curve.

I

Mr Lewis F. Day said, and with him I cordially agree, that there are two objections to striking : " The first is the inevitable hardness which results from geometrically struck lines, and the second is the constraint which the instrument imposes upon the invention of the artist." Mr Day would sketch in his design freely, as it occurred to him, until he obtained the effect that he wanted. He then set out mathematically with vertical and horizontal lines the obvious geometric divisions into which the design fell. The framework and scaffolding being set out, he added any radiating or other help lines as may

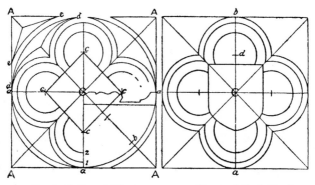

1. Quatrefoliated Circle.   2. Quatrefoiled Circle.

assist in subdividing, cusping, and so on, and then drew in firmly and finally, without recourse to mechanical instruments, the details of one repeat of the design. This repeat he traced and transferred to the other divisions which have been previously mathematically set out.

A knowledge of plane geometry is a great help to the student who intends to carve Gothic tracery, but the true artist invariably deviates from the hard and fast rules. In a purely geometrical figure like the *quatrefoliated* circle there is no objection to striking, and two methods are here given.

The working square of the quatrefoliated circle
(p. 2.1) is $7\frac{1}{2}$ in.; set this out on paper. Then draw
the diagonals AA, AA, and the diameters *aa*, *aa*, being
careful that they all pass through the centre point C.
Divide A to C into three equal parts, and set off one
of these divisions on the diameters at *a* to *c*. Join all
the points at *c* with straight lines. The angles (*c*) of
the diamond will be the centres for the *foliations*, the
inner curve being stopped by the diamond. The
quatrefoliations are composed of a flat band $\frac{1}{4}$ in.
wide and a hollow moulding $\frac{1}{2}$ in. wide. These
dimensions may be set off from *a* on the diameter
with an inch ruler, and *ca*, *c*1, and *c*2 will be the
radius for the foliations; C*a* the radius for the larger
or enclosing circle. With the same centre (C), and
an additional $\frac{1}{4}$ in. added to the radius C*a*, describe the
arcs *e*, *e*.

When the pattern is carved the enclosing circle is
stopped at *d*, *d*, as so fine a line would not be satisfactory if put in with a tool. A section of the carved
detail is given on the centre horizontal line from C to *a*.

Another method of setting out would be to bisect
the diameters from *b* to C, taking the point of bisection
d as the centre of the *foils* (p. 2.2).

In this case the curves would be more semicircular
than in p. 2.1, and the ground spaces would be larger.
This is sometimes an advantage, especially if a shield
has to be introduced.

Before cutting the outline of the *quatrefoil*, and to
prevent the wood from splitting, start in the middle
of the ground space, and with a large gouge make three
or four cuts, meeting each other in opposite directions
until a fair-sized opening is made. The outlines of the
compartment *c*2 may then be cut and the ground removed
(p. 62, Part I.) to the depth of nearly $\frac{1}{2}$ in. Next put

in the hollow with a flattish gouge, and finish off with a
quicker one. Note carefully how the grain of the wood
runs, and stop directly it begins to split, and work in
the opposite direction. The tools must be held very
firmly but not stiffly. A decided cut is essential ; at
the same time the wrist must be able to bend the tool
promptly to the curve required. When the hollows are
finished, put in the sunk pockets (p. 44, Part I.). Then
carve the central leaf.

The diamond forms the mass or boundary line for
the leaf, the shape being slightly humoured for the stalk.
The springing of the stalk from the moulded edge is a
difficult thing to carve, so unless the student has gained
some proficiency, he had better keep to the diamond
shape and treat it as shown on p. 40. The diagonal
lines divide the leaf into three lobes, with small ground
spaces between each. They need only be partially cut
away before the leaf is modelled. Make two or three
cuts on the diagonal line, first on one side and then on
the opposite side, so as to free the tension of the wood,
and then put in the hollows on either side of the lobes.
After this separate the calyx from the outer leaves, and
model the details. The outline may then be cut and
set in, and the ground finished.

The Littleham panels (p. 5) were probably not struck,
as they vary very considerably. If drawn freehand, it
would be as well to follow Mr Day's method, and to
trace the repeat of the ogee. These wave or ogee lines
form the basis of a very large number of patterns. The
Littleham panel starts at the top with two nearly completed circles, the circumference of which divides and
passes from the circle into the ogee or wave line. In
the centre of the ogee the bands merge into one at 3
(p. 6.1), and then again spring into two. To master the
difficulty of keeping the band a uniform width it is neces-

sary to start the setting out with a line in the centre of the band, which does not appear when the pattern is carved. This central line is merely a working line, from which

Details of Perpendicular Screen at Littleham-cum-Exmouth.
Fifteenth Century.

the necessary measurements have to be obtained, and is essential for all geometric patterns with bands.

In the diagram on p. 6, two geometrical methods of setting out the ogee pattern are given as a help to

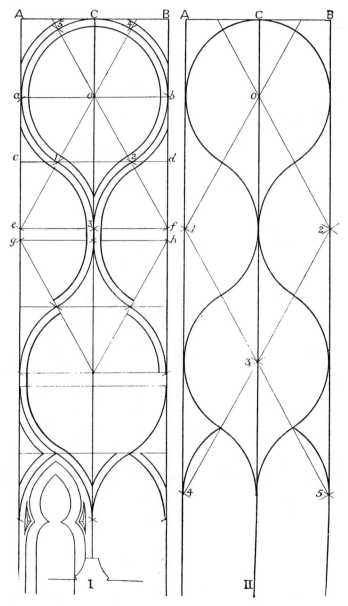

Diagram giving Two Methods of setting out the Ogee Wave Line.

the student to analyse the pattern. The Littleham panels follow No. I., whilst the more ordinary geometric basis is given in No. II. The curves of the ogee have been *stilted* in No. I., and the result is a flatter curve, which is more graceful than the fuller lines of No. II. In the diagram, B represents the centre line. Set out on paper the width of your panel, A, B, $5\frac{1}{4}$ in., and divide this into quarters with four vertical lines, marking the central line B and the quarters C. So far the same for both methods. In No. I., from C set off the distance C*o*, equal to CB, and from *o*, with the same radius describe a circle. Through *o* rule a line *ab* parallel with AB. From either *a* or *b*, and with the same radius, divide the circumference of the circle into six parts. Through points 1 and 2 rule a horizontal line *cd* parallel to *ab*. Through points 5 and 2, and 4 and 1, rule oblique lines until they cut the vertical lines A and B at *e* and *f*.

Through *ef* rule a line parallel to *cd*. With *f* as centre, and *f*2 as radius, describe the arc 2 3, and repeat the same at *e*. These points *f*3 2, and *e*1 3, when united, form equilateral triangles. Rule *gh* parallel to *ef* and $\frac{1}{4}$ in. from it. This allows for a straight piece between the curves, which is an advantage. The rest of the panel is set out in the same way. When the central ogee line is completed, $\frac{1}{8}$ in. is added on either side for the width of the band, and the curves are described from the centres previously used. The oblique lines mark where the curve on one side stops, and where it should be continued on the other side. For instance, *o* is the centre for the arcs from *b* to 2, and *f* is the centre for the arcs from 2 to 3. The lines are not completed below, so that the student may see how the various curves fit in. A section of the carving is given at I.

For No. II., B being the centre line, describe the circles, and mark their centres *o, o*. From each of these points (only one is shown in diagram), with *o, o* as radius, describe arcs intersecting the vertical lines A, B at 1 and 2. From these points, with the same radius, mark 3, and from 3 set off 4 and 5. Rule oblique lines through these points, when you will obtain a series of diamonds, each one being composed of two equilateral triangles set base to base. The angles of the diamonds are the centres for striking the curves.

Both methods of setting out are applicable to any sized circle, or any number of circles; but whatever the number may be, put in the circles first, and work from these downwards. The line AA then becomes the base line to work from.

In both the methods given (I. and II.) the pattern starts with two circles, and finishes off with a row of four small equilateral triangles. These form the heads of the narrow vertical compartments. These divisions may be of any length, according to the size of the panel. The dimensions of the right-hand panel of the Littleham example are 33½ by 5½ in. The one on the left is the same length, but rather broader. The small row of diamonds is not the centre of the panel, which is just above on the line of the cusps. The vertical compartments are repeated under these, and are the same height as those above; but instead of the inverted arches the upright members at the base abut on to a chamfered moulding, followed by a plain band about 1 in. wide. Below this is a quatrefoliated circle, with a leaf in the centre very similar to that on p. 1; but the corners of the square have foliage instead of the sunk pocket.

There is a very great variety in the panels of the screen, two variations being illustrated here. These are the only

examples of the kind I have seen, although at Llanegryn
(p. 88) the tracery panels are pierced and combined with
floral ornament. The combination is well worth considering, but the student must bear in mind that the
floral ornament must be so far removed from Nature as
to be in keeping with the arbitrary lines of the tracery.

In carving the
Littleham panels
only the tracery
would be at first set
out on the wood.
For the ornament,
the surface of the
wood between the
ogee lines should be
prepared to an ogee
curve, similar to one
of the sides of the
leaf given in section
on p. 85, Part I.
Refer also to the leaf
and diamond on p.
40. The details are
then drawn in and
carved. The back-
ground in the Little-
ham examples
slightly rises in the

Detail from Littleham.

centre, that is to say, the wood is cut roughly away and
not reduced to a dead level. This is a distinct advantage,
as a flat ground in tracery has a very mechanical effect.

Some of the panels at Littleham have arched heads
filled with tracery and foliations, and others have
tracery, foliations, and floral ornament alternating in
the geometrical divisions.

For the French example (given below) any sized panel could be used, the subdivision of the parallelogram being regulated, according to the dimensions of the panel. A repeating square can also be treated in the same way, but the lines are not so pleasing as when the opposite sides only of the parallelogram are equal. Set out on paper the size of your panel, and divide it into two parallelograms (pp. 11, 12). Draw the diameters

GOTHIC TRACERY, FRENCH.
Late Fifteenth Century.   Victoria and Albert Museum.
Reg. No. 1504-1904.

of each, and at the point of their intersection describe a circle. Where the circle cuts the diameters at 1, 2, 3 and 4, project tangential lines (the dotted lines in the diagram). In the spaces so obtained draw the required curves at 1 and 2 freehand.

It will be seen from the diagram that the central line of the bands is the first thing to set out, and that it represents the angle of the principal band. The next thing to do is to draw in the lines on either side of it, and then make a tracing and reverse it for 3 and 4. Transfer the measurements to the wood and trace on the pattern, which should be set out up to the stage of I. on p. 12. With an extra flat gouge cut vertically the wood on either side of the band, and round over the ground spaces as shown in section (II.). Next chamfer the edges of the band, which will complete the first order of the tracery.

The second order of the tracery is then traced on the wood. Fit a piece of tracing paper to the ground spaces of I. and II. Divide it in both directions by a central line and draw in the details, striking the semicircles with a compass if found easier. Trace the pattern on the wood. Many people would prefer, after having rubbed a little French chalk over the surface of the wood, to draw the details on the

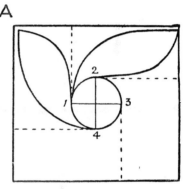

Diagram of French Fifteenth-Century Gothic Tracery.

wood rather than trace them as just described. The pattern would look better if the central angular band were wider ; the bands in the example are too much of one width. The rosettes are unsatisfactory, the gouge cuts being poor and ineffective, whilst the central shape also requires the cuts to be more strongly emphasised.

The treatment of the ground spaces is very unusual, and helps to enrich a somewhat simple design ; in a complicated design it would not be desirable. It seems possible, by the Frenchman's method of work, that the carver of the panel (p. 10) noticed the excellent effect of the bossed ground in its preliminary stage, and it may have recalled to him the nulls or gadroons (p. 58) of the silversmith's work, and so have decided him to depart from the recognised traditions. The silversmith's and the wood-carver's methods are so diametrically opposed, that the result is probably one of coincidence, rather than of imitation. Compare the method of working (p. 10) with the quarter repeat of a pattern (p. 13) taken from some English panelling in the Victoria and Albert Museum, and probably about the same date.

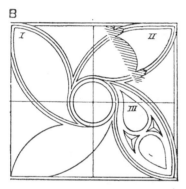

Diagram of French Fifteenth-Century Gothic Tracery.

In the French example the foliations lie on a curved plane (II.), which starts with a quirk from the band. In the English example the foliations are not quirked, and lie on a flat plane (p. 13, A). This constitutes a very radical difference between English and French and Flemish tracery. The foreign method is far less mechanical and far more pleasing than the one ordinarily pursued in England.

In the beautiful bench end from Lapford in Devonshire (p. 14) the first order consists of a round moulding (p. 13.2), which would be carved down to the dotted line before the foliations were set out on the wood, leaving the plane for the second order flat. The details should then be drawn in, the ground spaces cleared, and a *quirk* set in all round the pattern before running the hollow. The quirk when found in English tracery suggests foreign influence (see section, p. 13.2).

The bench end terminates in two quatrefoiled circles, the centres for the foils being a sixth of the diagonal as at p. 2.1. The carving at Lapford is strangely mixed up with Renascence detail, in which it seems likely that French workmen gave their rendering of Italian designs, and so probably influenced the English carvers.

1. ENGLISH TRACERY.

Late Fifteenth Century (?). Victoria and Albert Museum. No. 539-1892.

A purely English treatment of the rounded moulding used in tracery may be seen in the lower panels of the fifteenth-century rood screen at Chaddesden in Derbyshire, of which a section is given (figure 3). There is no quirk between the hollow and the flat, although the setting in of the bead gives a very necessary line of shadow. The tracery is pierced and applied, which was invariably the case in large work where the construction necessitated it. In the bench end this would not be necessary. When the panel is not too thick and can be let in to a framing, the tracery is far better carved out of the solid.

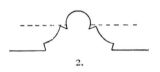

2.

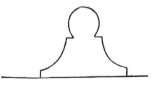

3. Section of Tracery, Chaddesden, Derbyshire.

A fragment of a very fine French flamboyant tracery panel is illustrated on p. 15. "The beautiful flamboyant tracery of the French came straight from the brain of the artist, modified only by the hand

BENCH END, LAPFORD, DEVONSHIRE.
Early Sixteenth Century.

FRAGMENT OF AN OAK PANEL.

Carved with the Arms of France amid Gothic Tracery.
French, late Fifteenth Century. Height, 2 ft. 3½ in. ;
width, 11 in. Victoria & Alb. Mus. Reg. No. 868-1895.

that drew it " (L. F. D.). This gives the charm to the
work.

An attempt has been made in the diagram (p. 18) to
set out the leading lines geometrically, but these do not
quite tally with the original, even if an allowance be
made for the cut of the tool.

The surface of the panel (see p. 15) appears to
have been slightly rounded over before the pattern
was drawn in, so as to obtain a higher relief in
the centre. The tracery is divided in three orders
(see section below). The first order is $\frac{1}{2}$ in. in relief,
broadly speaking, though here and there in the centre
it is as much as $\frac{5}{8}$ in. The second order is $\frac{3}{8}$ in. in

Section of Tracery enlarged from Diagram.

relief, and the third order $\frac{1}{4}$ in. in relief. This specimen
is unusually elaborate, as it is not often that
examples of Gothic tracery are to be found of three
orders.   Only a portion of the fragment is seen
on p. 15, whereas in the diagram above the whole
of it is given with a detail of the foliations. If
the student wanted to copy the panel he would
have to complete the lower part of it in a suitable
way. The diagram (p. 18) has been set out in the
following way :—

Mark off $12\frac{3}{8}$ in. by $7\frac{7}{8}$ in., which is smaller than
the original but the size of diagram, and divide this
by three vertical lines into four equal parts, A, B, C,
B, A.   Subdivide these, allowing a larger space for
the crockets than for the small arched vertical com-

partments. For these the only definite point is B, and this is the centre for the central compartment. Take the width of this (*bb*), and from B as centre on the inner line, with radius *bb*, describe an equilateral triangle, and repeat this for the other compartments Make AE equal to the altitude of two of these triangles, EF equal to five, and FG equal to EF.

Through E, F, and G, rule lines parallel to A, A. Within EF the principal arches are struck, the curves being formed by the bases of two spherical, equilateral triangles.

Join 2 and 3, and bisect the line at 5. From points 5 and 2, with radius 5-2, describe arcs intersecting at 7; this is the point from which to strike the upper curve of the ogee. From points 5 and 3, with the same radius 5-2, describe arcs intersecting at 4, which will be the point from which to strike the lower curve of the ogee. The other centres are found in the same way. These ogee lines form the central line, previously insisted on, of the angular ridge of the band of the first order. This band is $\frac{1}{4}$ in. wide, and the lines to complete it are struck from the same centres as the central line.

The line G divides the shield from the pointed arch below; the point where G intersects the central vertical line C is the centre for the radiating lines of the crown, and which, if carried through, gives the centres of the small arched compartments. The ogee lines in the divisions to the right and left are struck from equilateral triangles, the width of one side being equal to 8-9, as in the Littleham diagram, p. 6.1.

The first order of the panel comprises the ridge line of the principal ogee arches, some of the details of the crown, the fleur-de-lis on the shield, the crockets, the

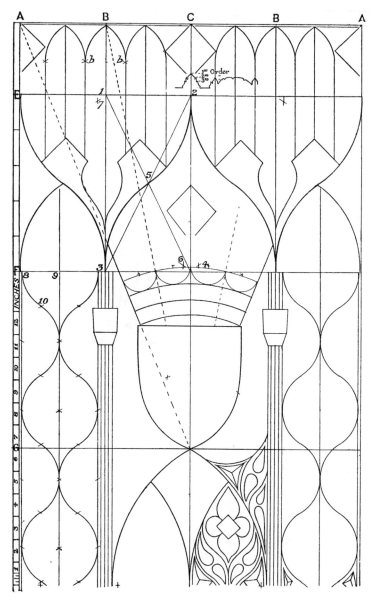

Geometrical Diagram of Panel on p. 15.

central part of the column and of the bands of the capital. When all these details are marked in, the ground should be cut away from the lines of the tracery to the depth of $\frac{1}{8}$ in., leaving the surface of the wood, in the details mentioned, intact.

The second order should then be put in; it comprises all the angular bands not included in the first order. The lines on either side of the bands should be cut down gradually to the depth of $\frac{1}{4}$ in., and the wood between rounded over, like section, leaving the central part of each compartment the same height as the ridge of the second order.

Doorhead, Carved with Tracery, Flowers, Foliage, and the Letter M. (Modern.)

The foliations belong to the third order, which is $\frac{1}{4}$ in. below the second order. The intermediate flamboyant divisions, not given in diagram, should be drawn freehand.

In France and Flanders the angular ridge in tracery is very common, whereas in England the flat band usually takes its place. This is rarely used on the Continent. The rounded moulding seems to have been popular everywhere and at all periods.

Gothic Tracery Panel.   French.
Late Fifteenth Century.

Pulpit at Kenton, Devonshire (restored).   Fifteenth Century.

Detail from Screen, Little Hempston.

CHAPTER II

GOTHIC CARVING (CONTINUED)

THE introduction of various symbols in the tracery also added considerably to the interest of the old work.

One of the earliest and the most universal of the Christian emblems was the fish. It was the symbol of water and of the rite of baptism.

It should be noted that the letters of the Greek word *Ichthus* (fish) contain the initial letters of the name and distinctive titles of Jesus Christ in Greek, *i.e., Iesous Christos Theon Uios Soter* (Jesus Christ of God the son, the Saviour). The symbol known as the Vesica Piscis or fish's bladder is frequently found in the tracery enclosing the figure of Jesus Christ.

The emblems of the four evangelists were also very popular, viz., the angel, the lion, the ox, and the eagle, and they were usually represented with wings. There are no very definite data to go upon as to when the four mysterious creatures mentioned in the vision of Ezekiel (chap. i.-v.) were first adopted as the emblematical symbols of the four Evangelists. In the seventh century they had become almost universal as distinctive attributes.

Vesica Piscis.

QUATREFOIL PANEL, FRENCH.

Oak, Carved in Relief with an Angel, the Emblem of St Matthew,
holding a Scroll. Late Fifteenth Century. Size, 9 in. by 9 in.
Victoria and Albert Museum. No. 675-1895.

According to St Jerome, St Matthew was symbolised
by the cherub, or angel, the human semblance, because
he begins his gospel with the human generation of Christ,
or according to others, because in his gospel the human
nature of the Saviour is more insisted on than the
divine. St Matthew was one of the apostles; he stands
first amongst the evangelists, because his gospel was the
earliest written.

QUATREFOIL PANEL, FRENCH.

Oak, Carved in Relief with a Winged Lion, the Emblem of St Mark,
holding a Scroll. Late Fifteenth Century. Victoria and Albert
Museum. No. 859-1895.

St Mark was not an apostle ; he is represented by the
lion, because he set forth the royal dignity of Christ, or
according to others, because he begins with the mission
of the Baptist—" The voice of one crying in the Wilder-
ness," and ends it fearfully with a curse—" He that
believeth not shall be damned."

Consequently the most terrible of beasts, the lion,
was appropriated as his symbol.

QUATREFOIL PANEL, FRENCH.

Oak, Carved in Relief with a Winged Ox, the Emblem of St Luke, and a
    Scroll. Late Fifteenth Century. Victoria and Albert Museum. No.
    858-1895.

St Luke was typified by an ox, because he dwelt
upon the priesthood and sacrificial work of our Lord.
The ox typifying the atonement for sin by blood. St
Luke was not an apostle, but according to some traditions
was a painter. In the Catacombs was found a crude
drawing of the Virgin, beneath which were the words,
"Una ex VII. a Lucos depictus" (one of seven painted
by Luke).

QUATREFOIL PANEL, FRENCH.

Oak, Carved in Relief with an Eagle, the Emblem of St John the Evan-
gelist, holding a Scroll.   Late Fifteenth Century.   Size, 9 in. by 9 in.
Victoria and Albert Museum.   No. 676-1895.

St John has the eagle, which is the symbol of the
highest inspiration, because St John soars upwards, to
the Divine nature of the Saviour.

St John was distinguished amongst the other apostles
as the Divine, the Theologian, the "disciple whom Jesus
loved."   In later years he was accused of magic and
exiled to the island of Patmos.   At the age of ninety he
wrote his gospel.

Of the French panels the winged ox is the least satisfactory. The lion is admirably carved. Note the simple massing of the hair and the feathering of the wings. Both examples of the eagle show an excellent broad treatment of the bird's plumage without any small realistic details. The angel too is well designed for the space it has to fill, and is executed in the same simple broad manner as the others.

The emblems are about 1 in. in relief, and the ground is sloped from the edge but is otherwise flat.

For a further study of this very interesting subject the reader is referred to Mrs Jameson's " Sacred and Legendary Art."

Foliage Gothic panels are not so common as tracery panels, but the one on p. 28 is a very fine example. The design is excellent, although the start of the foliage from the mouths of the grotesque birds is not altogether happy. The treatment of the carving is admirable in all but the branches, which are a little too round and not equal to the way in which they were treated by the Devonshire carvers of the same period.

The feathering of the birds is just what it should be for broad effect, and the thistles are well massed. Very typical of Northern French work is the manner in which the roots are treated. The background is punched, but so lightly and sparsely that it is hardly observable. The inner marginal lines are sloped towards the carving, which is half an inch in relief. The sight measure of the carved panel is 3 ft. by 2 ft.

In the lower part of the door are two linenfold panels, and they are very suitable in such a position. Simply treated, the linenfold pattern consists of a series of mouldings worked on a panel with the joiner's plane. In order to make the panel slide into the framing, the mouldings at either end had to be cut away from the

PANEL FROM A CARVED OAK DOOR, NORTHERN FRENCH.

Late Fifteenth Century.   Height, 3 ft. ; width, 2 ft.
Victoria and Albert Museum.   No. 853-95.

ground, and for better effect were cut back with a chamfer. This gave the effect of a folded surface, which probably gave rise to the name, and is far more probable than if it arose from the direct imitation of a folded linen cloth. The linenfold panel almost entirely supplanted the carved panel in Tudor times.

CARVING IN THE ROUND

A pinnacle is shown in process of carving in figures 1 and 2 on p. 30.

It is composed of five parts (see figure 3).

1. The finial or crowning member.
2. The collar or necking, which divides the finial from the crockets.
3. The shaft.
4. The crockets.
5. The gable (*e*).

Pinnacles were used in Gothic wood-carving for the termination of buttresses, gables, &c. The term finial is by some writers applied to the whole pinnacle, although it should be confined to the bunch of foliage which terminates a pinnacle, a canopy, or a pediment.

For carving in the round it is necessary to make a full-sized plan and elevation of the object about to be carved, whether it be a figure or a Gothic pinnacle. When all the necessary measurements are set out on paper, these then can be transferred to the wood.

To carve the pinnacle overleaf, procure a piece of wood 3½ in. square by 18 in. high. Set out on paper your plan, 3½ in. square, and from this project the elevation 18 in. high (3).

In carving a small detail like a pinnacle, a better idea is obtained of what is wanted by sketching the details of

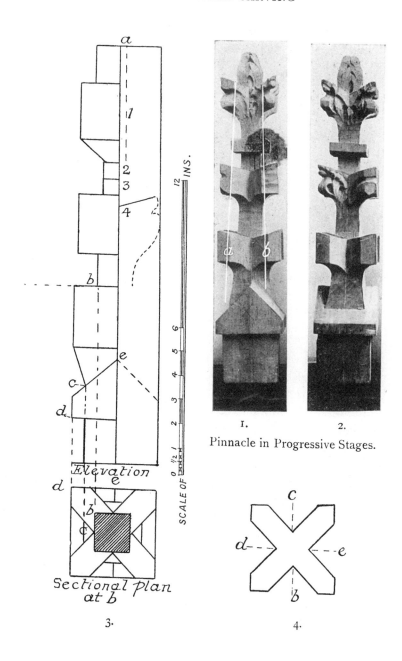

Elevation

Sectional plan
at b

3.

I.

2.

Pinnacle in Progressive Stages.

4.

the elevation first. Lines can then be projected from
these details on to the plan. Unless the student is
accustomed to geometrical drawing, he may find some
difficulty in understanding 3, p. 30. If all the dotted
lines are followed from the plan to the elevation,
and these are com-
pared with 1 and 2,
the student ought to
be able to follow the
method of work.

The elevation is
drawn from the pin-
nacle, showing one of
the pointed sides of
the gable, 1, p. 30.
The sloping side of
the gable is given in
2, p. 30. The dif-
ferences in the two
sides must be noted,
and a second eleva-
tion must be made
from the point *e* (3)
downwards, as the
student will require
to know exactly
where the wood has
to be cut away.

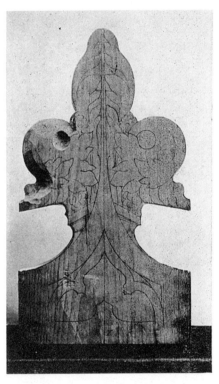

Poppy-head in Progressive Stages—I.

From the line *b*
in elevation, the plan is projected. It includes the
section of the shaft at *b*, represented by the central
shaded square. As the shaft descends so its size in-
creases, and this is shown at *c*, which is also the level
where the gable and shaft unite.

The projection of the crockets slightly diminishes as

the rows ascend. The first row below b is the square of the wood, $3\frac{1}{2}$ in.; the second row (4) is $3\frac{3}{8}$ in. square, and the top row or the finial (1) requires a square of $3\frac{1}{4}$ in. This diminution must be set out in the elevation. The plan and elevation being ready, the

next thing to do is to transfer the measurements to the wood. Rule a vertical line (a) down the centre of each face of the wood, and set out the lines given in elevation as well as those from the second elevation for the other side (2). The first shaping of the wood must be kept square, and the preliminary work can be done with a small saw and chisel. When the wood has been shaped to the square lines, the angular recess between a and b (1) must be made. Rule lines through a and

Poppy-head in Progressive Stages—II.

b (1) parallel to the outside edge, and 1 in. distant from it, and then cut the wood away between, as shown in 4.

Next put in the sloping lines of the crockets, as shown on the right-hand side of elevation (p. 30.3) at 4. The various stages of modelling are given in 1 and 2, and a completed crocket is shown on the left-hand side of 2.

The position of the eyelet holes should be carefully considered. They should be fairly large and deeply cut, so as to produce a strong shadow. Occasionally they are pierced, but this would depend on how the carving was to be lighted.

Poppy Head.   Poppy Head.
Fifteenth Century.   Modern.

For carving the pinnacle, symmetry and balance are the essential points to be considered, then follows detail.

The method of fixing, illustrated on page 3, Part I., would be found convenient for carving the pinnacle and for the poppy head (1 and 2, Part I.).

The term "poppy head" is applied to the terminating ornament of a Gothic bench or seat. It may be carved with crockets, leaves, figures, animals, &c., and is often extremely elaborate.

After the wood has been cut to the required shape, the central line or stem should be put in on each side with a V or veiner before the surface is disturbed, as it forms the backbone of the whole. The work in stages is shown at p. 31, and one side completed at p. 32.

The illustration from Hexham Abbey is a good example of Perpendicular or fifteenth-century wood-carving.

Note the treatment of the leaves which form the crockets of the gables, the battlements on the rail at the back, the mouldings and the segmental arch below.

Carving showing Crockets, Finials, and Panels from Hexham Abbey.

Pierced Detail from Screen, Llanrwst East.

CHAPTER III

MOULDINGS—GOTHIC

ANY architectural member is said to be moulded when the edge or surface of it presents continuous lines of alternate projections and recesses.

" A drawing which represents the outline of the projections and recesses is called the section or profile of a moulding, being the appearance it would present if cut through in a line at right angles to its bearing." *

The sections of Renascence mouldings, derived from Roman architecture, are given on p. 50. They are few in number and definite in their form, and introduced into certain positions and in accordance with established rules.

" In Gothic mouldings, variety of outline is no less essentially characteristic of the mouldings themselves than the frequency of their occurrence is characteristic of the Gothic style. Gothic mouldings appear in almost every conceivable position ; from the bases of piers and the piers themselves, to the ribs of the fretted vault which they sustain, scarcely a member occurs which is incapable of receiving consistent decoration by this most elegant method. In this multiplicity of moulding work the almost only combinations which are not commonly found are such as would have appeared to assimilate to, or to have been derived from classic

* Paley's " Manual of Gothic Mouldings."

Stall, Salisbury Cathedral, *c.* 1225.

authority. Such being the practice of the masters of Gothic art, we are disposed rather to assign to themselves the invention and development of their own admirable system of mouldings, than to seek its origin from another source." *

The dog-tooth moulding shown in the Salisbury example is the typical carved moulding of the Early English style, and the moulding before it is carved is prepared with chamfered sides, as shown in section.

Section.

It is then spaced out and cut into square pyramids, like the nail head ornament so frequently used in the first part of the thirteenth century. For the dog-tooth moulding, deep triangular cuts are made on the sides of the pyramid, so that the surface is

---

* Brandon's " Analysis of Gothic Architecture Mouldings," p. 48.

broken up into four teeth or leaves. These are sometimes flat, or are sometimes hollowed with a gouge. Both treatments are shown in the example from Salisbury.

Another very simple but effective enrichment which alternates with the dog-tooth moulding on the thirteenth-century stalls at Salisbury, is a series of two concentric incised circles, cut with a gouge on a slightly hollow moulding, and finished off on either side with a quirk and round moulding.

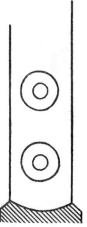

Detail from Thir-teenth - Century Stalls, Salisbury.

With this exception in Gothic woodwork only the convex mouldings are carved, and the carving always lies on a concave ground. The fullness of the curve varies considerably, but the larger members are rarely semicircular in section, although the smaller or dividing members usually are. The marked characteristics of the carved Gothic mouldings are the curved face of the carving, with the curve reversed for the background. As the style advanced the curves became flatter, until in the late Perpendicular work they became dull and uninteresting.

The patterns vary considerably, and in each style there are characteristic ornaments, which can easily be studied in books of Gothic ornament. Patterns, like the dog-tooth, the ball-flower, and other *motifs*, are carved continuously, or singly, or in groups, with a plain hollow space between, as in the Exeter screen.

The other enrichments consist chiefly of running patterns, of the foliage peculiar to the style, with figures, heads, animals, and birds introduced.

One of the finest examples of decorated or fourteenth-century Gothic is the Bishop's throne in Exeter Cathedral, erected by Bishop Stapledon in 1317. A detail is given from one of the niches which shows a

very characteristic treatment of the leaf. Compare this with the Kenton examples on p. 44, and with the still later mouldings from Lapford, p. 46, and Hexham, p. 34.

In the Exeter screen (p. 39.1), which is of the Perpendicular period, the mouldings are very shallow, and the curves much flatter than those of the preceding styles. The moulding is spaced out into squares, three being allotted to the centre; the pateræ are then carved, the wood removed between, and the ground slightly hollowed.

The cresting above the moulding is not nearly so interesting as the one on the doors of the transepts of the same cathedral (p. 39.2). The cresting is always carved out of a flat band, and is used not only as a crowning member, but often inverted so as to finish off a group of mouldings as at Lapford, p. 46.

Fourteenth-Century Detail, Exeter Cathedral.

The patera is so frequently used in mouldings and in its larger form of boss, to cover the intersections of the mouldings of the vaulted (p. 46) or the flat roof, that two varieties are given here.

One of the simplest forms of patera is on p. 40,

and the setting out of this is shown below at 2. Ornament with a serrated or broken edge should

1. Cresting from a Screen in the Choir of Exeter Cathedral.
Fifteenth Century.

be marked in, and grounded out, with a mass or boundary line as at *a*, and the principal undulations

2. Cresting from a Screen in the Transepts of Exeter Cathedral.
Fifteenth Century.

should be modelled, before drawing in, or carving the details.

Cut the lines of the diamond to the depth of $1\frac{1}{2}$ in. by easy stages, and slope the wood from the outer dotted

1. PERPENDICULAR PATERA, MODERN.
6 in. square by 2 in. thick.

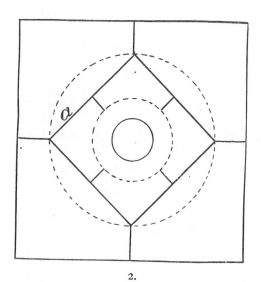

2.

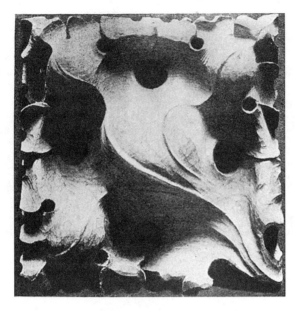

1. PERPENDICULAR LEAF, MODERN.
6 in. square by 2 in. thick.

2. ELEMENTARY STAGES OF LEAF.

circle to these lines. Next cut the circle in the centre
and waste away the wood from the inner dotted circle to
the centre one. To give the bend of the leaf, gouge a
deep hollow round the diamond in the direction of the

1. DETAIL OF OAK ROOD SCREEN.
Fifteenth Century.   South Pool Church, South Devon.

inner dotted circle, and repeat the process with the outside square. After this, pencil in the details. The eyelet holes, the four dark spots round the central rosette,

2. Section of
Larger Mould-
ing above.

and also where the diamond overlaps the
square, are grounded out very deep so
as to obtain a dark shadow.

Another pattern is given on p. 41.1,
the process of work being shown at 2.
It illustrates the usual method of carving a Gothic leaf. The dark spots have
been put in with a pencil, to show where
the ground has to be removed, in order
to form the eyelet holes. Sometimes
these were pierced, and then a drill was
used. Note the accentuation of the ogee line in 1. It is
still more apparent when the leaf is viewed in profile.
This is a marked characteristic of Gothic ornament.

In the beautiful example from South Pool, the large

member is applied. The wood is about $5\frac{1}{4}$ in. wide and about $\frac{3}{4}$ in. thick, and is prepared like b in section. The moulding, carved and pierced and in its original state, was probably attached to the background a or casement moulding, leaving a space between the carved surface and the background. This was sometimes flat and sometimes curved. After the Reformation the screen was taken down, and was found some years ago in a very mutilated condition. The fragments were nailed up and placed together until funds were forthcoming to restore it. This has now been done. The illustration was taken before the restoration, and does not give the original grouping of the mouldings. The main features of the principal moulding are the waved line of the stalk, which is $1\frac{3}{4}$ in. wide, the vine leaves 6 in. square, with their strongly marked ribs, al-

ARCH MOULDINGS AT
DARTMOUTH.

Fifteenth Century.

ternating with the delicately carved tendrils, and the counterchange of light and dark masses produced by the perforation. This latter effect is only to be obtained in

PERPENDICULAR MOULDINGS FROM THE PULPIT AT KENTON, DEVONSHIRE.
Fifteenth Century (?).

this way, and was not an expedient for saving time or material. The twists and turns of the tendrils are the spontaneous fancy of the carver, not any two of them being quite alike. Very similar details are to be seen at Portlemouth (South Devon) with still more elaborate interlacements, and the fine screen at Dartmouth forms one of the same group. The interlacements are carried out in the arch mouldings at Dartmouth, and in many of the inverted crestings, as at South Pool, which

DETAIL FROM BACK OF SCREEN, LAPFORD, NORTH DEVON.
Early Sixteenth Century.

would have been placed below the other members. It is 5 in. wide.

The three fragments from Kenton are carved with a conventional treatment of the vine, the leaves showing marked fifteenth-century Perpendicular characteristics. The front or convex side of the moulding is in section about two-thirds of a circle, it is pierced and applied to the casement, similarly as the example given from South Pool. The corrugations of the stalks and tendrils is a very noticeable feature in all Devonshire work, and one the student should not fail to observe. These delicate lines give light and shade to the carving and a variety to the surface, which when simply rounded over looks hard and uninteresting. The grapes, too, are treated much in the same way, small facets being left on the surface so as to diffuse the light and shade.

A very popular ornament during the fifteenth

PORTION OF A ROOD SCREEN, LAPFORD, NORTH DEVON.

Early Sixteenth Century.

century is the leaf and stick moulding. The South Pool example is $2\frac{1}{2}$ in. wide. It is the one very commonly used for the arch mouldings, but at Lapford, North Devon, the enrichment round the arches is the same as the lower member of the detail from the back of screen. The carving on the arched mouldings is worked out of the solid, and the ground is concave. The carved portions would have had more value had some plain surfaces been introduced.

This fault is observable in most of the Devonshire screens, but notwithstanding this there still remains so much to admire that we may justly be proud of the carving, which is indeed quite unique.

No finer examples of carved wood Gothic mouldings

Cresting and Band from a Modern Screen.

can be found than those at South Pool, Portlemouth, Dartmouth, Kentisbere, Lapford, Kenton, and in many other remote corners of Devonshire.

Some of the screens in Somersetshire and Norfolk are also very striking, but for beauty of design and skill in treatment they cannot be compared with the South Pool group.

Jacobean Border—Modern.

CHAPTER IV

MOULDINGS CONTINUED (RENASCENCE AND JACOBEAN)

MOULDINGS serve a very definite purpose in cabinet work, and when used intelligently are not merely ornamental additions.   Wood is greatly affected by temperature, its tendency being to contract or shrink in a dry atmosphere.   The moulding fitted round the lid of the French chest (p. 27.2, Part I.) not only keeps the surface of the wood from twisting, but also helps to exclude the dust by lapping over the top rail.   If the wood were to shrink and the joint to open, A, being slightly higher than the lid, would help to disguise the opening of the joint.   When two flush surfaces are brought together a bead is often a most useful addition.

Mouldings should be varied in width and section, and should be grouped together so as to form distinct lines of light and shade.   For internal work they should not have much projection, as, if a line of shadow is required, the moulding can be quirked or undercut.

The classic entablature, consisting of cornice, frieze, and architrave, has formed the basis of all the later mouldings, and can be easily recognised in Renascence and Jacobean work.   The cornice, reduced to its simplest elements, consists of three mouldings, not counting the fillets, the frieze, of a band either flat or convex, the latter called a "pulvinated frieze"; and the architrave, which was originally composed of three fascias divided by a moulding, is usually a group of two mouldings and a fascia.   The term architrave is now applied to the mouldings round the opening of a fireplace, round a window and a door.

The classic entablature in the Renascence period was not strictly adhered to, although the main divisions of cornice, frieze, and architrave were never lost sight of.   The crowning mouldings of the cabinet on p. 62 exemplify this.

The sections of the principal mouldings used in cabinet work are given overleaf.   They are, with the exception of the thumb moulding, the same as were used by the Romans, who adapted them from the Greeks.   The student should make himself familiar with their names.

The fillet is a small flat *member*, and is used to separate one curved moulding from another.   When the flat is sufficiently wide to form a distinctive feature it is called a fascia.

The cyma is, as its name implies, "wave-like" in profile.   It is composed of a concave and convex curve. In the cyma recta the concave curve is uppermost, and in the cyma reversa this is reversed.   In cabinet work the "cyma" is commonly called "ogee," from the French *ogive*, an arch of double curvature.

Two methods are shown for striking the cyma : the first, A, by quadrants of circles, struck from an angle of a square ;   the second, *a*, from equilateral spherical triangles, in which the wave-line is formed by the bases of the triangles.   When the cyma recta is carved, the less acute curve of the equilateral is recommended, but when it is plain the fuller curve gives more light and shade.

The smaller cyma reversa is *quirked*, that is to say the moulding and the fillet are both chamfered off and form a small angular recessed channel.   The two mould-

ings do not make a right angle, as in the examples
above it.

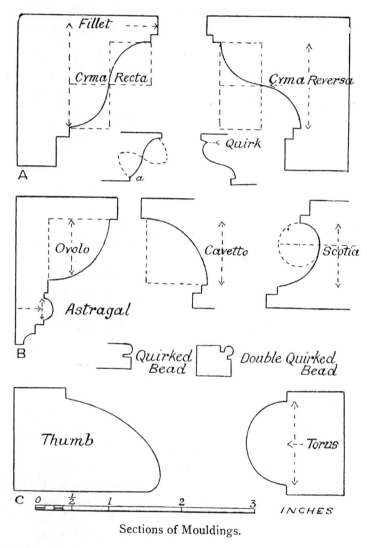

Sections of Mouldings.

The cyma recta is usually carved with the acanthus
leaf, water leaf, &c. (p. 53); but the cyma reversa, when

large and used as a crowning member, is more often left plain.

The ovolo or quarter round should, as its name implies, be enriched with the egg and tongue, although the ovolo in Jacobean and French work is often carved with a variety of simple gouge-cut patterns. The egg and tongue ornament should never be carved on any other section but an ovolo.

The cavetto is also a quarter round, but struck the reverse way to the ovolo. The cavetto is useful when a deep shadow is required. It is rarely carved, the curve of the moulding presenting many difficulties to the carver. A carved example may be seen on the fireplace in the Jerusalem Chamber at Westminster, date 1624.

The scotia is a very effective base moulding, and is composed of two quarter rounds, the larger one being twice the radius of the smaller.

The torus is a half round, and looks well when carved.

The astragal is a smaller torus, and is sometimes called a bead. It sometimes is used instead of a fillet. A bead, according to Rickman, should not project beyond the fillets on either side.

The thumb moulding is purely a joiner's moulding, and is suitable for the lids of chests, tables, &c. It lends itself to various carved treatments.

Repose requires that some mouldings should be left plain ; if all were enriched, confusion would arise and not variety.

In woodwork the square members or fasciæ are sometimes carved, but great discretion should be used in the choice of their enrichment. Dentils are the most suitable form of decoration, the flat band being divided up into small blocks with a recessed space between.

The ornamentation of mouldings should be simple and uniform, and should not combine more than two distinct forms or *motifs* in the repeat. These two *motifs* should vary in size, and should be cut to the same depth so that an uninterrupted appearance is preserved. The egg and tongue moulding is an exception to the uniform depth of cutting, but the contour of the moulding and the unity of the whole is well maintained.

Mouldings with patterns that are grounded out are not very satisfactory. If they are used the background should have the same section as the surface of the moulding.

The saw-cut line on the left-hand side of p. 53 shows where the mitre joint will come. It should be slightly cut or scratched on the moulding before it is carved, leaving a little extra wood for the final planing, when the mitred sides will be glued together.

In carving a moulding the first thing to do is to determine the repeat of the pattern A, B (p. 53).

For the egg and tongue moulding rule a vertical line on the wood, and apply the section of the moulding, p. 50, B, to this line and use it as the repeat. This will give the outer curve of the band enclosing the egg. In repeating the pattern allow a small space between the curves for the upper part of the tongue. Sketch two repeats on the wood to form a complete pattern. If the lines are not pleasing, correct them before proceeding further. It is better to do the first sketch on the wood, as the pattern, being on a moulded surface, no adequate idea can be formed of it when drawn on paper. A little white chalk rubbed over the surface of the wood makes it easier to draw on.

The next step is to see that the repeat will fit properly into the length of wood which has to be carved. Measure the length of the moulding from the lower corners of the mitre, divide this in half, and rule a line down the centre. From this centre line, with a pair of spring dividers, space off the width of your repeat, which

1. Egg and Tongue Moulding.   Section B, p. 50.

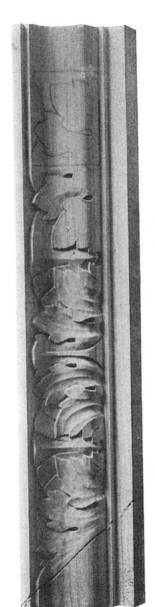

2. Acanthus Leaf Moulding.   Section A, p. 50.

should end at the mitre line with a little less than one repeat—that is to say, if the repeat is $1\frac{1}{4}$ in., like the pattern, and the length of the moulding was 4 ft. $3\frac{3}{4}$ in., you would get from the centre line twenty repeats = 25 in., and $\frac{7}{8}$ in. over at the mitre—a little more or less would not matter. The best treatment is to carve the mitre as illustrated, with half an egg and a leaf, the stem of the leaf being left the full surface of the moulding so as to get a good joint at the mitre. This necessitates starting with an egg in the centre. The mitre leaf should not be too small. If, however, the piece of moulding were only 4 ft. 2 in., then it would take exactly twenty repeats (from the centre) without anything to spare at the mitres. The following points would then have to be considered :—

1st, By starting with an egg in the centre, the half egg would be brought up right to the corner of the mitre, which would not be satisfactory.

2nd, By starting with a tongue in the centre you would finish off with a tongue and a leaf overlapping the band.

This makes the mitre too solid and does not look well.

The wisest course to pursue would be to keep to the same number of repeats, but by decreasing each a fraction, $\frac{3}{4}$ in. might easily be obtained for the mitre leaf. An infinitesimal fraction, repeated on a long length, makes a very appreciable difference at the end.

When the repeats have been measured out, the lines A, B should be ruled in with a card, bent to the curve of the moulding, and all the centres of the eggs marked with an X, so that there shall be no error before drawing them in.

In other mouldings students can take any length for the repeat they think suitable, and by dividing the length of the moulding by the width of the repeat, will easily see how it fits in.   To avoid the fractions of an inch, two or more repeats can be taken for the dividing number.

For $1\frac{1}{2}$ in. divide by 3 in. (2 repeats).

„ $1\frac{1}{4}$ in.   „   5 in. (4 repeats).

„ $1\frac{1}{8}$ in.   „   9 in. (8 repeats).

These would, of course, have again to be subdivided.   It will be found very helpful to calculate out the divisions on paper first, and then work by the results on the wood. The details of the ornament having been decided on, they should be set out on paper in the following manner :—

Fit a piece of tracing paper to the curve of the moulding and trace the pattern drawn on the wood. Rule in the lines of the repeat on the tracing paper, and superimpose these on the corresponding lines on the wood, and insert carbon paper as before described (p. 53, Part I.).   The tracing should be cut to the width of the wood, allowing a little extra on either side of the lines A, B for convenience in tracing.   When a long length of moulding is set out, directly the tracing is blurred a fresh one should be used.   Two repeats so as to form one complete pattern should only be used.

If the pattern is first drawn on paper, instead of on the wood, measure the curve of the moulding with a strip of paper, and set out the width of it on your drawing paper, by ruling two horizontal lines the width of the curve apart.   Decide on the repeat, and erect two per- pendicular lines A and B for the same ; between these two lines draw the repeat of your pattern, which on paper will look somewhat elongated, and from this make your tracing.   The various stages of carving the egg and tongue are shown in the illustration (p. 53).

First, the outline of the egg is separated from the enclosing band by a small fluter.   Next, the outline of the egg is cut, care being taken not to allow the tools to slope inwards. The wood is then sloped from the inner line of the band to the egg ; after this, the egg is rounded over with a gouge, which should fit the curve of the egg. Work with the inside of the tool to the wood. The full surface of the wood should be left in the centre of the egg, where the repeating line is drawn. Never obliterate this with the tools. The eggs should always be carved first. The tongues may then be cut and the band finished off with a gouge, leaving a small flat on either side.

The bead and astragal below should centre with the egg and tongue. It is advisable to arrange the astragal at the mitre, as it forms a stronger surface for the joint than the bead. The beads are spaced out the width of the moulding. These spaces are then separated with a chisel, and afterwards rounded over with the inside of a gouge, which should exactly fit the curve of the moulding.

The section of the carved acanthus leaf moulding (p. 53) is given at A, p. 50. It will be noticed in the section, that under the top fillet there is a small flat band before the ogee moulding begins ; this projection is requisite when the moulding is carved, so as to allow for the relief of the ornament. When it is not carved it is treated like the section given on p. 65. The width of the moulding, measured along the mitre line of cyma, forms a very good width for the repeat. The stems should be left the full surface of the wood, and the one at the mitre should not be cut until after the angles have been glued together. The position of the stem till then should only be indicated with a veiner. The setting out, drawing, and tracing of the pattern would be the same as described for the ovolo. The space at the mitre should be equal to one repeat or a very little less. It does not look well to have the ornament contracted at the mitre.

The first leaf on the right shows the preliminary work, after which the stems are put in. They should be started with a veiner, and then cut down, care being taken not to undercut the wood where it is weak. The leaf should then be modelled, and the smaller serrations cut in after this. The curve of the background at the top must be preserved.

Section C (p. 50) is a popular moulding with the cabinetmaker, and is called the "thumb moulding." The term is also used by the trade for the gouge-cut patterns found on Elizabethan and Jacobean furniture (6 B, p. 43, Part I.).

The section given at C is only suitable in a horizontal position, and placed below the eye, as, for instance, for the edge of a table or a chest. For a simple carved treatment the gouge-cut pattern on p. 48, Part I., would do well. The more general way of treating section C is to carve it into *nulls*, as 1 on the page overleaf, which is a fragment of an old seventeenth-century moulding. If the section were slightly adjusted by the addition of a fillet on the outside, the pattern below of the French moulding (2) could be carved on it. The section of this, given on p. 59, would only be suitable as a crowning member. The moulding is troublesome to set out, as the lines of the repeat must be curved and not straight, and at first only the *gadroons* should be marked in. These should be cut round, and the spaces between grounded out to the dotted line in section. The bands and leaves should then be drawn in and the ground recessed round the gadroon. Model these in the same way as described for the eggs on p. 56, leaving the full surface of the wood down the centre of the gadroon. The pattern radiates on either side of a central heart-shaped boss, and the mitres are finished off with a leaf.

1. OAK MOULDING, ENGLISH.   Seventeenth Century.   Section C, p. 50.

2. WALNUT MOULDING, FRENCH.
Seventeenth Century.   Victoria and Albert Museum.   No. 1942-1904.

The projecting moulding above is also set out obliquely, but radiates in the opposite direction to the gadroons. The ornament consists of a small angular channel, similar to that between the gadroons, but instead of being finished off with a leaf, it is pointed like a tongue. The small ovolo at the top is not enriched.

These gadroon mouldings were much used in Italy at the beginning of the sixteenth century, and were introduced into England during Elizabeth's reign. They became very popular in the seventeenth century. The official label describes the French moulding as seventeenth century ; there is, however, no reason why a similar carved moulding should not have been found in France a century earlier, but then the section of the mouldings at the top would have been different. The spacing out of frames, either moulded or plain, is a troublesome matter. Mr Hugh Stannus in one of his very interesting lectures on design, given at the National Art Training College, gave the following suggestions, which are very helpful.

SECTION OF FRENCH MOULDING (p. 58.2). Half Full Size.

If the dimensions of the width and length of your frame are such that the same number will divide both the short and the long side, the dimensions are then said to be " commensurable." For instance, 20 in. by 16 in. can be divided by 4 in. This would give five repeats on the long side and four repeats on the short side, of 4 in. each.

When two numbers cannot be divided by the same factor, then they are termed "incommensurable," as 24 by 17. In this case, take half the width of the shorter side, which would be 8½ in., and set this off from either

end of the long side, when a space of 7 in. in the middle
would be left. From both ends of this central space of
7 in. set off the same measurement as is left in the
middle, so as to have three repeats of 7 in. ; these may be
again subdivided, if a smaller repeat is required, into six
repeats of 3½ in. ; 1½ in. will be left at each angle for
the mitre. On the short side there will be two repeats
of 7 in., or four repeats of 3½ in., with the same space of
1½ in. for the mitre as on the long side. The spaces left
at the angles will all be of the same size, but slightly
smaller than the repeat. This cannot be avoided, and
for a frame it is generally an advantage, as it gives a
feeling of strength to the pattern, which has always to
be adapted to the mitre joint.

If the student will set out on paper some commensurable and incommensurable numbers and test these
methods, he will very soon see how they work.

Carved frames are not always mitred, as sometimes
a mortice and tenon joint suits the design better. The
treatment of the corners has then to be made in accordance with the construction, so as to cut into the joint as
little as possible. A square ornament, leaving a margin
to cover the joint, is the best, but this limits the scope of
the designer. When possible, the student should avoid
cutting into the joints, otherwise they will open out, and
not only will they lose their strength, but will look very
unsightly (pp. 20, 21, Part I.).

In heavy picture-frame mouldings it is advisable to
have the lowest square member of the moulding made
separately and framed up, as shown in section on p. 61,
with simple mortice and tenon joints. The mouldings
are mitred and planted on the face of the flat frame. It
should project a little beyond the edge of the moulding.
The square jointed frame underneath, which can be
square or hammer-headed, like the one on p. 61, is of

great assistance in keeping the mitre joints from opening, especially when the mouldings are heavy.

The beautiful frame of carved mouldings on this

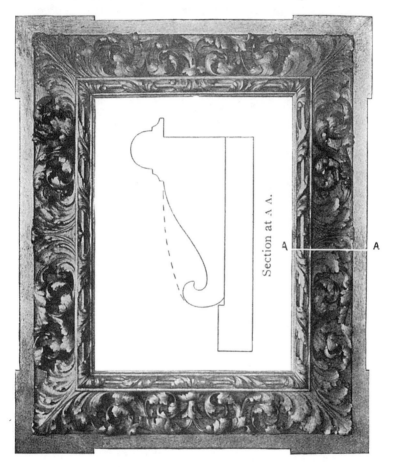

Section at A A.

ACANTHUS LEAF FRAME.
Carved by the late W. H. Grimwood.

page is, however, much more elaborate than any of the
moulding previously given, and cannot be worked in the
same way.

The carved mouldings are of lime, and are planted on to a walnut back. The larger moulding is pierced, but this can only be done in process of carving. The section given is taken through the centre of the acanthus leaves at the side A. The dotted line shows how the wood is shaped previous to carving; the leaves in some places being the full height of the wood.

The stems and turnover of the central leaves to right and left follow the curve of the continuous line in section. The curve of this and of the dotted line must always be kept in mind as the work proceeds, and the bosses and general curves must first be bosted in and then follow the details, similarly as described for the Spanish pilaster.

CABINET, CARVED CHESTNUT
WOOD, FRENCH.

About 1560. Victoria and Albert
Museum. No. 2573-1856.

The details of the ornament are beautifully drawn, and are carved with astonishing grace and vigour. Such a piece of carving should only be attempted by an expert.

Speaking generally, the enrichment of mouldings for furniture cannot be too simple, and no better examples can be found than those of the Henri II. style in France.

A portion of a French cabinet is given above, in

which the treatment of the mouldings is admirable.   In no case has the contour of the moulding been disturbed by the enrichment, which consists principally of gouge cuts.   The mouldings are admirably suited to the strapwork of the period.

Each historic style has its own distinctive mouldings and enrichments, but the subject is too vast to be dealt with adequately here.   The student must therefore observe, and make sketches and notes for himself.

Some of the mouldings given on p. 50 will be seen grouped together in the section (p. 65) of an Italian bracket (overleaf).   The bracket is carved with an oblong panel between two volutes, the panel being enriched with an oval boss and a leafy border, and the scrolls with flutings and stems bearing leaves and fruit ; the whole is surmounted by a projecting cornice decorated with bands of leaf and fluted ornament.   The crowning member of the cornice is a plain cyma recta, with a fillet at the top, and separated by another fillet from *a*, which is a cyma reversa or ogee.   This member is carved into a simple leaf; the repeat or outline for the leaf is taken from the section of the moulding. The central stem is incised and carved like a sunk pocket (p. 44, Part I.).   The outline of the leaf is cut and the wood sloped to the outline from the little triangular space which is left up.   Below *a* comes the fascia *b*, which might also be described as the dentil band.   The dentils are separated from each other by a small sinking, and on each dentil there is a flute.   The underside of *b* is called the "soffit."   The ovolo at *c* has a very simple enrichment.   The small crescent is made with two cuts of a gouge.   The waved line underneath it is set down with a gouge, and the wood sloped from the semicircular line to the cuts.   The triangular spaces of the second *motifs* are grounded out, and the husk cut to the outline

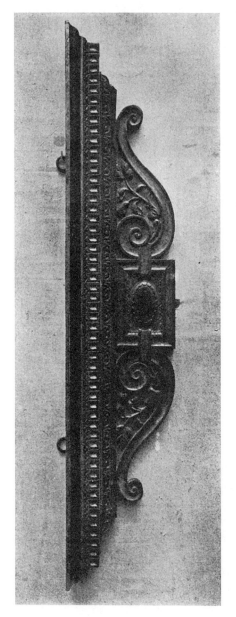

BRACKET OF WALNUT, PARTIALLY GILT, ITALIAN.

Sixteenth Century. Height, 10¾ in. ; width, 4 ft. 1¾ in. ; depth, 6⅛ in.   Bought.
Victoria and Albert Museum.   No. 494-1897.

and rounded over. The underside of the scrolls at *d* is carved with rectangular pockets *d*.

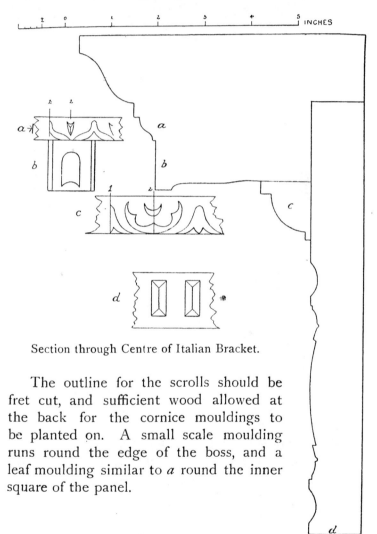

Section through Centre of Italian Bracket.

The outline for the scrolls should be fret cut, and sufficient wood allowed at the back for the cornice mouldings to be planted on. A small scale moulding runs round the edge of the boss, and a leaf moulding similar to *a* round the inner square of the panel.

Detail from an Italian Renascence Cabinet.   Sixteenth Century.

CHAPTER V

RENASCENCE CARVING

THE teaching of advanced carving cannot be adequately treated in a book, all that can be done in it is to suggest the best way to set to work.   Renascence carving as a means to obtain technical dexterity is a splendid training, but for the advanced work the carver needs to be an artist as well as a craftsman

By far the best period of Renascence carving for the student to study is the continental of the sixteenth century.   The lines are simple, and the surface of the ornament is not worried.   The frontispiece and Spanish pilaster are fine examples.   By the end of the seventeenth century the carving became more complex, as will be seen in the examples in the last chapter.

The acanthus leaf and the spiral line are the principal *motifs* to be found in the designs, therefore, as a preliminary study, the student is advised to work out the leaf on p. 68.

The treatment of the acanthus leaf varies considerably in the different periods, as will be seen by comparing an example of the François I. style with examples of the Louis XIV., XV., and XVI. styles.

The study illustrated on p. 68 is a modern example, somewhat after the style of Louis XVI.   This form of leaf is known as a sheath leaf, *i.e.*, it protects or sheathes the stalk, which in a Renascence design

66

would probably work out into a spiral. The design should be traced on the wood, and each lobe or principal division of the leaf should be massed in with a plain line (p. 39). It is to this outline that the wood should first be cut away, in the manner described in Part I. The left-hand side of the leaf being in very low relief, the wood is considerably lowered before the details are drawn in. The lowest lobe on the right-hand side shows the preliminary stages of modelling, the one above, a further advance, whilst the lobe at the top is completely finished. A small veiner may be used for marking in the details on the left-hand side. These smaller lobes should die off in parts into the background, and nowhere should they be too detached. A good-sized fluter is very useful for defining the central veins. These lines exemplify the principle of radiation. The highest parts of the relief are about $\frac{3}{8}$ in.

After the relief is roughly modelled in, mark in the serrated edges. Make a straight cut between the serrations, and work from the points on either side, into the cut previously made ; that is to say, cut from where the wood is weak to where it is strong. Note that these curves are nowhere rectangular. The leaf can then be undercut and the ground finished off.

A detail of the beautiful Spanish panel is given on p. 69. The left-hand side shows how the work is first blocked in, then follows the detail. From this it will be seen that in elaborate carving much of the detail has to be drawn in as the work proceeds. To attempt to cut in the fine spiral from the top surface of the wood would be quite futile. When the wood has been lowered to the depth required, it is far better to vein the outline of the spiral than to cut it down. When the veiner is used the student is able to correct any bad

Acanthus Sheath Leaf in Progressive Stages.

Detail in Progressive Stages of Spanish Panel, Oak.

1. Renascence Panel in Italian
Walnut, Spanish.

Sixteenth Century. Length, 24¾ in. ;
width, 9⅞ in.   Victoria and Albert
Museum. No. 573-1893.

2. Copy of Spanish Panel
in Progressive Stages, Oak.

Carved by C. White
(School of Art Wood-Carving).

line which when once cut is irredeemable. The relief
of the carving is $\frac{5}{8}$ in.

By the side of the original a copy is shown in
various stages of progress. By comparing the two
together the student will see how such a piece of
carving is carried out. The original is in Italian
walnut, which is much better suited to the design
than oak, which has too much figure. The panel is
enclosed in a moulded frame, the inner mouldings only
being shown in the illustration.

The construction of the Renascence bracket on the
page overleaf is much the same as that on p. 64,
only the carving below the cornice (line AB) is out of
3-in. stuff, and is $14\frac{1}{2}$ in. deep. A thin board would
have to be let in and screwed at the back, behind the
cornice, so as to reduce the weight. It is $3\frac{1}{2}$ in. high, and
although the mouldings are bolder, the section is very
similar to that on p. 65, except that the ogee member
at a is omitted.

Parts of the scrolled ends of the panel, the boss and
the cherub's head, are the full height of the wood, which
is just under 3 in., and this during the process of carving
is reduced to $\frac{1}{4}$ in. for the central part of the background of the strapwork cartouche. This is slightly
curved, and so is the scrolled panel beneath it, owing to
the treatment of the panel out of which it is carved.
These variations can be readily detected by a careful
examination of the illustration.

The bracket has been adapted for a hat rack. The
pegs are turned, and project $6\frac{1}{2}$ in., which is unnecessarily high. They are in no way part of the design,
and the upper pegs detract considerably from the effect
of the scrolled ends. The original is clumsy, and an
adaptation on a smaller scale would be much more
satisfactory.

HAT RACK, ITALIAN.

Walnut wood, carved in the centre with an oval boss, which divides an oblong strap-work cartouche, resting on a panel with scrolled ends. Above the boss is a mask, and beneath a cherub's head. The whole is surmounted by a projecting cornice of classical design. There are four pegs for hats. Sixteenth century. Length, 4 ft. 7¼ in. ; width, 17¾ in. ; depth, 6⅝ in. Victoria and Albert Museum. No. 18·1891.

An interesting detail for the carver is the capital
or crowning member of the shaft. It may be circular
or polygonal, according to the plan of the shaft.

A capital for a pilaster is given on p. 74, and for a
column on p. 75.   The floral swag in the late seventeenth-
century example is carved separately, and is attached
with screws to the capital, and the astragal is omitted.

The capital is composed of three members: the
abacus or supporting member, which is usually moulded ;
the bell, on which the ornament is carved ; and the

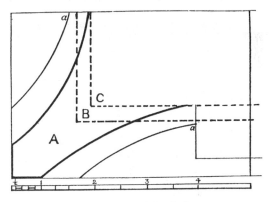

Half-Plan of Capital.

astragal or moulding which covers the joint between the
shaft and the capital.

Two important points to remember are that the
base of the bell should be the same size as the top
of the shaft, and that no part of the ground of the bell
should go below the face of the column of the pilaster.

The front and side views of a Renascence capital
are given in various stages (see figure, p. 74). It was
carved out of a block of yellow pine (9¼ by 3 in.) at
the School of Art Wood-Carving, South Kensington,
under the supervision of Mr Herbert Grimwood.

A half-plan of the capital is shown above.

Renascence Capital carved by Katie Miller.

Rule a centre line on each face of the wood, and draw on the top of the wood block the compartment marked A, which is bounded by a thick line. This is the plan of the abacus, which coincides in the centre with the dotted line C. Then mark in the lines a, a, which allow for the projection of the ornament on the abacus and on the sides of the bell. On the bottom of the block mark in the base C, and gauge a line on the front face and on the sides, $\frac{1}{4}$ in. from the lower edge, and waste away the wood, until the base C is left $\frac{1}{4}$ in. in relief.

This forms the astragal, B on plan. Waste away the wood with gouges from the compartments marked A—A and then proceed to block out the carved detail as shown in the progressive stages of illustration.

Late Seventeenth-Century Renascence Capital.

CHAPTER VI

LETTERING

DURING the last few years there has been a much-needed revival in the art of lettering, in all the branches of the arts and crafts.

In the woodwork of the Middle Ages lettering is a conspicuous feature, and we find names and inscriptions interwoven with the design, or the principal features of the design.

The letters on the Lapford bench end (p. 14) should be noted, not only for their shape and treatment, but for the interpenetration of the letters, which is a distinctive feature of the design. The background of the shield on which the initials lie is slightly curved, and the greatest projection of the letters is about $\frac{3}{8}$ in. The initial letters are those of Thomas Arundel, one of the patrons of the living. There is a good deal of variety in the lettering of the other bench ends, one T branching out into masks with foliage. This elaboration is not as successful as p. 14, which indeed could hardly be improved upon. The Renascence feeling in the treatment and design of the letters is kept in perfect harmony with the Gothic details, of which they form a part.

Thomas Silksted was the last Prior of Winchester Cathedral, and in the agitated times of the sixteenth century he left his diocese and sought refuge at

Shanklin, where he deposited in the old church the chest illustrated on the page overleaf. It is believed that he intended when, as he hoped, the Church was triumphant, to remove it back to Winchester, but he died at the old Manor House of Apse, near Shanklin, and his hopes were never realised.

The inscription round the border runs thus : " Thomas Silksted, Prior, Anno Dni. 1512. Dohphus." The margin of the border is sloped on each side towards the centre, where the letters are nearly ⅜ in. in relief. The surface of the letters is slightly hollowed with a flat gouge, and a few small punched or drilled holes are put in where emphasis is wanted. The centre panels bear the owner's initials, and in these the Renascence style has asserted itself. The date coincides with the year that Pietro Torrigiano came to England to consult with Henry VII. about the monument the king wished to be placed in Westminster Abbey.

The ground is sloped from the margin of the panels to the depth of nearly ½ in. in the centre. The design of the ornament is not all that could be desired, although there are some good details like the pendants from the buds ; the left-hand one is enriched with gouge cuts, and the one on the right with beads or " pearls," as they were called in the Romanesque period, when they were a very popular enrichment ; they are always effective in carving. The scheme of the lettering is excellent, but the carving both in the border and in the panels is too high in relief, and the margin for the depth of the relief is too narrow round the centre panels, and consequently looks weak and ineffective.

Very little later in date is the beautiful " M " on p. 79. The grace and simplicity of the carving must be seen to be fully appreciated. It is carved in Italian walnut, and is ⅜ in. in relief. A deep hollow runs round

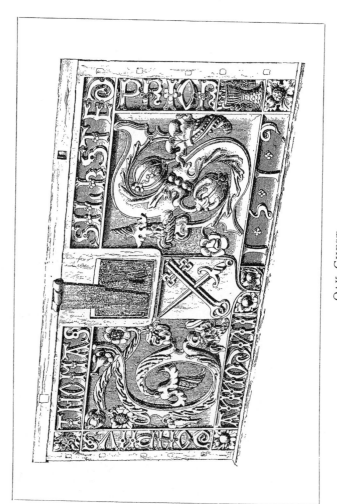

OAK CHEST.

In the Old Church at Shanklin.   Dated 1512.

the margin and dies off into the ground. The sub-
divisions of the panel are good, and the mouldings are
worked out of
the solid. The
c o m p a n i o n
panel, an " A,"
is in the Vic-
toria and Albert
Museum, No.
849 - 1895. Mr
Lewis F. Day
has illustrated
it in his book
of " Lettering in
Ornament," p.
162.

Simpler in
style is the " P "
from a fragment
in the Maison
Cluny, Paris (p.
80.1). It is
carved in oak,
and is $\frac{3}{8}$ in. in
relief.

More Gothic
in feeling are
the letters I.H.S.
from the bench
end at Trull,
although they
are considerably

PANEL, FRENCH.

Carved with the M(arie). First half of Sixteenth
Century. In the Museum of Science and
Art, Dublin.

influenced by the coming style. There is room for
improvement in the loop of the H, which looks like
an after-thought, and not part of the design. The

roughly punched ground greatly detracts from the carving.

1. From an Inscription in the Maison Cluny, Paris. Sixteenth Century.

A punched background was introduced towards the end of the fifteenth century, and afterwards became very popular. It is often an expedient used to cover the cuts carelessly made on the background, and consequently for this use should not be put into the hands of a beginner. Simple and fancy punches when employed to decorate a band, as in the sampler, p. 43, Part I., are useful, and also in lettering, as in the Silksted chest, but for a background their use is rarely justified. In the delicate Renascence panels of the sixteenth century at Perugia, opinions differ as to whether the punched ground does not detract from the carving rather than give value to it. The modern method of covering the whole ground with a finely pointed punch entirely separates the ornament from the ground, and is strongly to be condemned. One rarely sees a punched ground in French

2. From a Bench End at Trull. Early Sixteenth Century.

carving, and the relation of the ground to the carving is more keenly appreciated by the French carver than by the English or Italian.

There is a very interesting old beam in the Victoria and Albert Museum, No. 204-1900. The letters are flat and are about 2 in. high. The ground is lightly punched, but the dots are not very close together.

On either side there is a little chip-carving border as on p. 82.1, and the carving rises in parts and gives an agreeable break in the margin. Mr Lewis F. Day has included the letters of the inscription in his recent edition of " Alphabets Old and New."

In the two excellent examples on p. 82, executed at the School of Art Wood-Carving under the direction of Mr George Jack, the old beam above referred to has undoubtedly furnished suggestions. In " Beauty is Truth " (No. 1) the words are in relief on what is termed a cushioned ground, that is to say, the wood is only in part removed from the spaces between the letters, which are about $\frac{1}{16}$ in. in relief. The outline is veined, one side of the fluter forms the side of the letter, and the other angle of the fluted line is rounded off and merged into the surface of the wood, which is disturbed as little as possible. When the letters are free of the margin as in No. 1, the cushioned background is specially suitable, and also for a variety of designs in which the outline is broad and simple, and economy of labour is desirable. The value of plain surfaces is well illustrated in No. 2. Not only do the bands emphasise the lines, but they give value to the carving, and provide a surface to which the letters can be attached. Omit these details and remove the whole of the ground from the letters, and the result would be commonplace and unsatisfactory.

Another important point to notice in the design is the skilful way the background of the foliage is arranged in the word GOD. If the letters were cut away the spaces left would clearly show what the letters were. The ornament in the unlettered spaces adds to the

1. Designed by George Jack and Carved by Beatrice Smith.
Width, 2 ft. 5 in. ; height, 5 in.

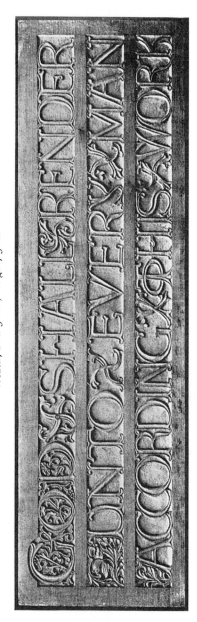

2. Designed and Carved by Maria E. Reeks.
Width, 3 ft. ; height, 10¾ in.

The besy larke the messager of day
Salueth in hir song the morwe grey
And firy phebus riseth up so bright
That al the Orient laugheth of the sight

Designed and Carved by Beatrice Smith.

Width, 2 ft. 3¾ in. ; height, 7¾ in.

enrichment of the design, and is rather Byzantine in treatment. These ornamental spaces are often of great value when the inscription has to be pulled out to fill a certain space, and the combination of the letters, like the " to " in p. 82.2, is equally useful when a contraction is needed. The introduction of a smaller letter, to fall in with the top line of the letters of a word, is also another expedient.

The letters and the ornaments are about $\frac{3}{16}$ in. in relief in Miss Reeks' example (p. 82.2). The ground was almost entirely removed with a fluter and a flat gouge, and only the breaks in the letters and the small serrations of the leaves have been set down.

In quite another style is the quotation from Chaucer on p. 83. The relief of this is $\frac{1}{8}$ in.

The selection of the alphabet entirely depends on the way the carver intends to treat the letters, or the style of the design.

The tendency of the carver is to give too much relief to the letters, and when this is the case they are liable to look hard and coarse, and be out of scale with their surroundings.

Words and inscriptions may mar or make a design, and consequently are of far more importance than the average student realises.

Broadly stated for a carved memorial tablet, the letters should be simple and uniform in size, so as to keep the inscription in line. These lines should be close together, without bands between, and the letters should be kept in low relief. The letters on the Trajan column are an excellent basis to work upon.

Detail from Screen, High Ham.

CHAPTER VII

PIERCED CARVING

IN pierced work the wood should be of a substantial thickness, otherwise it looks poor, and is suggestive of the veneered wood which is fret cut and carved.

The carver should always mark in on the wood the openings he wants made by the saw-cutter. They should always be well outside the line of the ornament, otherwise if the saw-cut has been set in there may not be enough wood for the required curve and the whole design may be spoiled. Many carvers prefer to start the openings themselves with a drill rather than trust the piercing of the wood to other hands.

During the process of carving, the wood should be glued to a board, as described on p. 18, Part I. Unless it is securely fixed it is liable to break.

In a church where the light is uncertain and the effect of the carving has to be considered from many positions, the Gothic method of piercing the carving and setting back the ground so as to leave a space between it and the ornament, as in the mouldings from South Pool and Kenton (p. 44), well deserves the carver's attention.

It is by this method that the carved panels in the pulpit at Coleridge are so effective, although the carving is so simple and likewise the construction. The pulpit is hexagonal in plan, and on each of the sides are two inclined boards about ¾ in. thick, perforated and carved.

The length of the panel where the boards are fitted together is 15 in., and the width of it is 5½ in. The lower ends are shaped to an ogee line, and are moulded and cusped, and a small triangular piece of wood, 8½ in. wide, is fitted in at the bottom and thrown forward.

The panels are held in position by the small upright members carved with overlapping leaves.

UPPER PART OF PULPIT AT COLERIDGE, DEVON.
Late Fifteenth Century.

The cornice contains some of the old carved mouldings, but the pulpit was restored in 1903.

The same effect has been obtained in the pierced panel on the next page, designed by Mr Lewis F. Day. It forms the front of a canopy over a niche, and comes forward about 8 in. By excluding the light on three sides, a depth of shadow is obtained in the background, which lends charm and mystery to the work. The broad sweeping lines of the design come out admirably in the carving, and there is much the student may learn from the design.

A very important point in pierced work is the distribution of the voids and solids. The ornament must on

Designed by Lewis F. Day.   Carved in Oak by Ellen Dakin.

no account be weak because it is pierced, and consequently where strength is desired, either from necessity or for effect, the voids should be small.

In the panel above, the wood is 1 in. thick, and is slightly chamfered at the back. The depth of the chamfer greatly depends on the position of the works.

In panels which are to be placed near to the eye, as

pp. 91 and 92, the chamfer is about $\frac{1}{4}$ in., and in some parts rather more.

In the Llanegryn examples the voids and solids are fairly evenly distributed, but a more subtle effect can be obtained by the designer if the ornament is massed together in certain parts, as Mr Lewis F. Day has done

PIERCED PANELS AT LLANEGRYN.
Late Fifteenth-Century Gothic.

in the centre of his design. In this central mass the larger leaves at the bottom form a background for the smaller leaves at the top, and by this means an intermediate tone is added between the light on the surface of the ornament and the depth of the shadow, where the ground is cut away. Variety is given to the rest of the design by balancing the outside of the leaf with the

inside of the leaf, so that there is a counterchange of
convex and concave surfaces.

By the end of the fifteenth century, the Gothic style
was practically dead, and the sixteenth century saw the
dawn of the early Renascence. The details from St Cross

PANEL FROM A CHANCEL RAIL, FORMERLY IN
WINCHESTER COLLEGE CHAPEL.

Late Seventeenth Century.

show the new style, with a faint echo of the Gothic in
the arch and the chamfer. By the end of the seventeenth
century the later Renascence was at its zenith in
England, and the panels from Winchester College
Chapel are very fine examples of this style. Note how
skilfully the foliage is united to the surrounding mouldings, and the strength that this gives to the design.

CANOPY OF A STALL, ST CROSS, WINCHESTER.

Early Sixteenth Century.

DETAILS FROM THE STALLS AT ST CROSS, WINCHESTER.

Early Sixteenth Century.

About the same period is the Flemish door, but it is very much simpler in treatment.

The character of the foliage and the small circular flat flowers are very typical of late seventeenth-century work.

CUPBOARD DOOR, FLEMISH.

Oak, decorated with a shaped compartment carved in openwork with symmetrically arranged leafy scrolls bearing acorns and flowers. Seventeenth Century. Victoria and Albert Museum. No. 859-1898.

It is carved out of $\frac{5}{8}$-in. stuff. The lines are bold and sweeping, and although the carving is simple, it is very deftly executed.

A very beautiful example of the later Renascence

LOWER PART OF PANEL FROM A CHANCEL SCREEN, FORMERLY
IN WINCHESTER COLLEGE CHAPEL.

Late Seventeenth Century.

UPPER PART OF PANEL FROM A CHANCEL SCREEN, FORMERLY
IN WINCHESTER COLLEGE CHAPEL.
Late Seventeenth Century.

style in England is as follows. The panel has been
divided so as to give the detail as large as possible, but
the student should have no difficulty in fitting the two
illustrations together. The strength, the grace of line,
the beauty of the carving, could not be surpassed ; more-
over, no one feature takes a central place, which adds
greatly to the interest of the design. If we may venture
to criticise, the treatment is rather too suggestive of the
ironwork of the period, which is very fine.

The Dutch example is the same in style, but the
foliage is more coarsely treated. The coat of arms
is admirably composed with the ornament, and the
lettering is excellent.

PANEL FROM A CHURCH SCREEN. OAK. DUTCH.
About 1700. Victoria and Albert Museum. No. 429-1901.

Border from an Italian Chest.   Sixteenth Century.

CHAPTER VIII

TREATMENT AND DESIGN

THE word treatment has been so frequently used in the foregoing chapters that it may be as well to state clearly what is comprehended in the term.   It is used to express the craftsman's rendering of a design, with due regard to position, material, and tool, so that the carving may satisfactorily fulfil the conditions required.

It is this very necessary convention that the carver is apt to lose sight of.   He is carried away by what he knows he can accomplish, rather than by the thought of what he wants others to see when the work is in place.

The treatment of natural forms is a very vexed question, but if the carver's aim is only to produce a realistic representation of Nature, he will never succeed. Colour has to be eliminated, and the carver has to concentrate his attention on line and form.   The serrations and the veins of the leaves, the plumage of birds, the hair on the skins of animals, and even the details of the human form have to be generalised to meet the limitations of the material.

These points the student must study for himself, and in the illustrations that follow he will have plenty of material to work upon.   He must, however, bear in mind that details, so as to give them as large as possible for the carver's benefit, being detached from

CARVING BY GRINLING
GIBBONS AT BELTON.
Late Seventeenth Century.

their surroundings, give no idea of the general effect. It is only possible to give a few examples of Grinling Gibbons' work, but it can be seen in St Paul's Cathedral, St James, Piccadilly, Kensington Palace, Hampton Court Palace, in many of the city churches built by Sir Christopher Wren, as well as in many of the English country seats.

The student must not take for granted that all the carving attributed to Gibbons is by his own hand, so that in studying his work it is well to keep to authenticated examples.

The example from Belton is unquestionably the work of Gibbons, but there is no authenticated document to prove that he was at work there, nor can the name of the architect be given with certainty, although the mansion contains all the characteristics of Wren's work. The existing building was built in 1685 on the site of a simpler

CARVED FIREPLACE, HAMPTON COURT PALACE. GRINLING GIBBONS.
English. Late Seventeenth Century.

CARVED DOORWAY IN THE KING'S GALLERY, HAMPTON COURT PALACE.
GRINLING GIBBONS. English. Late Seventeenth Century.

and less pretentious manor, which had belonged to Richard Brownlow. Gibbons delighted in Nature, and he carved whatever came to hand, be it flowers, leaves, fruit, birds, or fishes, and interspersed these with delightful winged Amorini, rarely showing more than the head. Delicate as his carving was, it was never weak ; and the little tendrils of wheat, foliage, flowers, and birds' wings were generally carved separately, and fitted into the mass of carved detail. At Belton some of the birds' wings project as much as 12 in.

The characteristic feature of Gibbons' work is that it is almost always executed in lime wood, and is applied to the background, which is generally of a different wood. The ornamental detail is usually carved out of three layers of wood, super-

PORTION OF A DROP. GRINLING GIBBONS.
In the Drawing-Room, Hampton Court Palace. English.
Late Seventeenth Century.

imposed one on the other, to the amount of the relief required. We find Gibbons working with Wren at Hampton Court in 1699 on the five rooms leading out of the guard-room. These contain some of his finest and most characteristic work.

The carved mouldings are very rich in effect, although simple and direct in the way they are cut, and the contour of the moulding is never lost sight of. The example on p. 99 is part of one of the drops on the right-hand side of the Duchess of Austria's portrait. The upper half of the drop is composed of further bunches of flowers, two singing doves piping to a winged Amorini above them, and finished off with further leaves and flowers, all exquisitely carved and graceful. The way Gibbons groups his masses and the carving of the same are essentially his own. With all his love of realism his work is broadly treated. He did at times rather overload his design, and for this reason I do not like the pierced panels of the screen at Trinity College, Oxford, as well as those from Winchester College, or the pierced altar rail doors at Chelsea Hospital, as much as the pierced altar rail panels from Winchester, which are more gracefully designed, and look better at a distance. Gibbons' work at St Paul's Cathedral, executed about 1695, is confined entirely to the choir, and as a complete whole is very fine.

The last authenticated carving of his is the panel from the chapel at Hampton Court, date 1710. The contrast of the plain surface of the bay leaf with the modelled surface of the oak leaf is very satisfactory, but the stems and ribbon knot have not the freedom of the earlier work.

Considerable interest is attached to the carvings which were formerly in Winchester College Chapel. Two expert carvers, well acquainted with the work

CARVED PANEL OF OAK LEAVES AND
BAY LEAVES. GRINLING GIBBONS.
In the Chapel, Hampton Court Palace. Date 1710.

of Grinling Gibbons, pronounced some years ago that
they were not his work, and dated them about 1670.
See p. 103.

CARVED TRUSS BENEATH THE GALLERY IN THE LIBRARY IN
ST PAUL'S CATHEDRAL. JONATHAN MAINE.
English.   Late Seventeenth Century.

It will be remembered that it was in 1671 that
Evelyn discovered Gibbons, working at Deptford, and
that it was some few years later before he received any
important commissions.

TWO DROPS, FORMERLY IN WINCHESTER COLLEGE CHAPEL.
English.   Late Seventeenth Century.

Mr H. Avray Tipping, M.A., F.S.A., in his most interesting book entitled "Grinling Gibbons and the Woodwork of his Age (1648-1720)," confidently attributes the Winchester College carvings to the time when Wren was supervising work at the College in 1684, but he does not think Grinling Gibbons was the carver, as some of the characteristic touches of his work are wanting. The carvings are all executed in

CARVED PANEL OVER THE DOOR TO CHANCEL (REPAIRED),
FORMERLY IN WINCHESTER COLLEGE CHAPEL.
English.   Late Seventeenth Century.

oak. Whoever was the carver, the examples are very fine, and the drops in their proper setting could not be surpassed. The panel of the oak leaves and the palms shows the same contrast of surface as was noted in the panel from the Chapel at Hampton Court Palace.

The French were consummate masters in the way they handled Nature. No better example could be found for low-relief treatment than the Louis XVI. panel in the Victoria and Albert Museum.

PART OF AN OAK PANEL, FRENCH.
Period of Louis XVI.   Late Eighteenth Century.   Victoria and Albert
Museum.   No. 960-1900.

In conclusion, a few examples of modern work are given. The panelling, designed by the late Lewis F. Day, shows the value of a plain surface. The carving is placed just where it will be best seen, the lower part

Designed by Lewis F. Day.   Carved by Ellen Dakin.

CARVED PANEL IN WALNUT—DEER FEEDING.
Designed and Executed by Muriel Moller.

Border Designed and Carved by Joseph Phillips.

being left plain, as a background for the various objects to be placed on the mantelshelf.

A very beautiful example of what might be termed " pictorial carving " is illustrated in Muriel Moller's " Deer Feeding." The pictorial element is strictly subservient to the material, and the trunks of the trees are so designed that they have the effect of supporting columns. The deer and the foliage are broadly carved without any attempt at detailed realism.

The border designed by Joseph Phillips gives quite a different carved treatment to any previously illustrated. The design is practically made during the process of carving, and this necessitates the carver being a designer as well as a draughtsman. The treatment is excellent for a narrow space, as a richer effect can be obtained than when the pattern is grounded out.

Let me urge upon the student to make careful studies of plant form, birds, animals, and figures, for it is only by going back to Nature that the Arts and Crafts will be virile and enduring.

GLOSSARY OF A FEW TECHNICAL TERMS USED IN THE TEXT

Cusp.—The ornament used in the tracery of Gothic windows, screens, wall arcades, &c., which forms the termination of the "foils" (Rickman).

Foils.—The arcs on either side of the cusps.

Foliated.—A foiled arch placed within a plain arch.

Foliations.—Sometimes known as "featherings." Professor Willis, in his "Architecture of the Middle Ages," p. 45, says, "There is a manifest distinction between 'foiling' an arch and 'foliating' it. In the first case the arch itself is indented into a number of small arches (or foils); in the second case such a foiled arch is placed below it" (the arch itself). The same treatment and terms are applied to circles and panels, pp. 1, 26. Professor Willis would have described the panel on p. 26 as "multifoil," with the foils alternately round and angular. This term is very rarely used.

Gadroon or **Godroon.**—The term is applied to the embossed mouldings of silver, and similar mouldings carved in wood are called by the same name (p. 58). The term is derived from the French word *godron*, meaning "a round plait"; see also "Null." R. Cotgrave's Dictionary (1611): "Goderon, a fashion of imbossment used by Goldsmiths, &c., and termed knurling."

Null or **Knull**=a bead. This term should only be used when the nulls are on centres perpendicular to two parallel straight lines; when the centres radiate, or taper inwards, or are drawn on mitre lines within two parallel lines, the long oval shape produced is the true Fr. Godron. Both the mouldings on p. 58 should be described as Gadroon or Godroon. The term null is often misapplied by English workmen to several varieties of ornament.

Nulled Work.—Ornamental turned work resembling nulls or beads, strung on a rod.

Order.—In Gothic Architecture the term order is applied to each plane of an arch, and is similarly used for the different levels of the tracery.   In an arch the innermost and narrowest order is spoken of as the first order ; in tracery, the outermost and thickest order is the first (p. 16).   The term in Classic Architecture is applied to the column with its entablature.

Quatrefoil.—See p. 2.

Quatrefoliated.—See p. 2.

Rebate.—A plain square sinking on the edge of a board or panel.

Spandrel or **Spandril.**—The triangular space between the outer mouldings of two contiguous arches or circles, or parts of circles, with a horizontal moulding or band above them.

Stilted.—The term is applied to an arch which has the capital or impost mouldings of the jamb below the level of the springing of the curve.   In No. I. diagram (p. 6), the arc C C is stilted, that is to say, it starts from a short vertical piece.

GENERAL INDEX

A CATALOG OF SELECTED DOVER
BOOKS IN ALL FIELDS OF INTEREST

CONCERNING THE SPIRITUAL IN ART, Wassily Kandinsky. Pioneering work by father of abstract art. Thoughts on color theory, nature of art. Analysis of earlier masters. 12 illustrations. 80pp. of text. 5⅜ x 8½. 23411-8

ANIMALS: 1,419 Copyright-Free Illustrations of Mammals, Birds, Fish, Insects, etc., Jim Harter (ed.). Clear wood engravings present, in extremely lifelike poses, over 1,000 species of animals. One of the most extensive pictorial sourcebooks of its kind. Captions. Index. 284pp. 9 x 12. 23766-4

CELTIC ART: The Methods of Construction, George Bain. Simple geometric techniques for making Celtic interlacements, spirals, Kells-type initials, animals, humans, etc. Over 500 illustrations. 160pp. 9 x 12. (Available in U.S. only.) 22923-8

AN ATLAS OF ANATOMY FOR ARTISTS, Fritz Schider. Most thorough reference work on art anatomy in the world. Hundreds of illustrations, including selections from works by Vesalius, Leonardo, Goya, Ingres, Michelangelo, others. 593 illustrations. 192pp. 7⅛ x 10¼. 20241-0

CELTIC HAND STROKE-BY-STROKE (Irish Half-Uncial from "The Book of Kells"): An Arthur Baker Calligraphy Manual, Arthur Baker. Complete guide to creating each letter of the alphabet in distinctive Celtic manner. Covers hand position, strokes, pens, inks, paper, more. Illustrated. 48pp. 8¼ x 11. 24336-2

EASY ORIGAMI, John Montroll. Charming collection of 32 projects (hat, cup, pelican, piano, swan, many more) specially designed for the novice origami hobbyist. Clearly illustrated easy-to-follow instructions insure that even beginning papercrafters will achieve successful results. 48pp. 8¼ x 11. 27298-2

THE COMPLETE BOOK OF BIRDHOUSE CONSTRUCTION FOR WOOD-WORKERS, Scott D. Campbell. Detailed instructions, illustrations, tables. Also data on bird habitat and instinct patterns. Bibliography. 3 tables. 63 illustrations in 15 figures. 48pp. 5¼ x 8½. 24407-5

BLOOMINGDALE'S ILLUSTRATED 1886 CATALOG: Fashions, Dry Goods and Housewares, Bloomingdale Brothers. Famed merchants' extremely rare catalog depicting about 1,700 products: clothing, housewares, firearms, dry goods, jewelry, more. Invaluable for dating, identifying vintage items. Also, copyright-free graphics for artists, designers. Co-published with Henry Ford Museum & Greenfield Village. 160pp. 8¼ x 11. 25780-0

HISTORIC COSTUME IN PICTURES, Braun & Schneider. Over 1,450 costumed figures in clearly detailed engravings–from dawn of civilization to end of 19th century. Captions. Many folk costumes. 256pp. 8⅜ x 11¾. 23150-X

STICKLEY CRAFTSMAN FURNITURE CATALOGS, Gustav Stickley and L. & J. G. Stickley. Beautiful, functional furniture in two authentic catalogs from 1910. 594 illustrations, including 277 photos, show settles, rockers, armchairs, reclining chairs, bookcases, desks, tables. 183pp. 6½ x 9¼. 23838-5

AMERICAN LOCOMOTIVES IN HISTORIC PHOTOGRAPHS: 1858 to 1949, Ron Ziel (ed.). A rare collection of 126 meticulously detailed official photographs, called "builder portraits," of American locomotives that majestically chronicle the rise of steam locomotive power in America. Introduction. Detailed captions. xi+ 129pp. 9 x 12. 27393-8

AMERICA'S LIGHTHOUSES: An Illustrated History, Francis Ross Holland, Jr. Delightfully written, profusely illustrated fact-filled survey of over 200 American lighthouses since 1716. History, anecdotes, technological advances, more. 240pp. 8 x 10¾. 25576-X

TOWARDS A NEW ARCHITECTURE, Le Corbusier. Pioneering manifesto by founder of "International School." Technical and aesthetic theories, views of industry, economics, relation of form to function, "mass-production split" and much more. Profusely illustrated. 320pp. 6⅛ x 9¼. (Available in U.S. only.) 25023-7

HOW THE OTHER HALF LIVES, Jacob Riis. Famous journalistic record, exposing poverty and degradation of New York slums around 1900, by major social reformer. 100 striking and influential photographs. 233pp. 10 x 7⅞. 22012-5

FRUIT KEY AND TWIG KEY TO TREES AND SHRUBS, William M. Harlow. One of the handiest and most widely used identification aids. Fruit key covers 120 deciduous and evergreen species; twig key 160 deciduous species. Easily used. Over 300 photographs. 126pp. 5⅜ x 8½. 20511-8

COMMON BIRD SONGS, Dr. Donald J. Borror. Songs of 60 most common U.S. birds: robins, sparrows, cardinals, bluejays, finches, more–arranged in order of increasing complexity. Up to 9 variations of songs of each species.
Cassette and manual 99911-4

ORCHIDS AS HOUSE PLANTS, Rebecca Tyson Northen. Grow cattleyas and many other kinds of orchids–in a window, in a case, or under artificial light. 63 illustrations. 148pp. 5⅜ x 8½. 23261-1

MONSTER MAZES, Dave Phillips. Masterful mazes at four levels of difficulty. Avoid deadly perils and evil creatures to find magical treasures. Solutions for all 32 exciting illustrated puzzles. 48pp. 8¼ x 11. 26005-4

MOZART'S DON GIOVANNI (DOVER OPERA LIBRETTO SERIES), Wolfgang Amadeus Mozart. Introduced and translated by Ellen H. Bleiler. Standard Italian libretto, with complete English translation. Convenient and thoroughly portable–an ideal companion for reading along with a recording or the performance itself. Introduction. List of characters. Plot summary. 121pp. 5¼ x 8½. 24944-1

TECHNICAL MANUAL AND DICTIONARY OF CLASSICAL BALLET, Gail Grant. Defines, explains, comments on steps, movements, poses and concepts. 15-page pictorial section. Basic book for student, viewer. 127pp. 5⅜ x 8½. 21843-0

CATALOG OF DOVER BOOKS

PERSPECTIVE FOR ARTISTS, Rex Vicat Cole. Depth, perspective of sky and sea, shadows, much more, not usually covered. 391 diagrams, 81 reproductions of drawings and paintings. 279pp. 5⅜ x 8½. 22487-2

DRAWING THE LIVING FIGURE, Joseph Sheppard. Innovative approach to artistic anatomy focuses on specifics of surface anatomy, rather than muscles and bones. Over 170 drawings of live models in front, back and side views, and in widely varying poses. Accompanying diagrams. 177 illustrations. Introduction. Index. 144pp. 8⅜ x11¼. 26723-7

GOTHIC AND OLD ENGLISH ALPHABETS: 100 Complete Fonts, Dan X. Solo. Add power, elegance to posters, signs, other graphics with 100 stunning copyright-free alphabets: Blackstone, Dolbey, Germania, 97 more–including many lower-case, numerals, punctuation marks. 104pp. 8⅛ x 11. 24695-7

HOW TO DO BEADWORK, Mary White. Fundamental book on craft from simple projects to five-bead chains and woven works. 106 illustrations. 142pp. 5⅜ x 8. 20697-1

THE BOOK OF WOOD CARVING, Charles Marshall Sayers. Finest book for beginners discusses fundamentals and offers 34 designs. "Absolutely first rate . . . well thought out and well executed."–E. J. Tangerman. 118pp. 7¾ x 10⅝. 23654-4

ILLUSTRATED CATALOG OF CIVIL WAR MILITARY GOODS: Union Army Weapons, Insignia, Uniform Accessories, and Other Equipment, Schuyler, Hartley, and Graham. Rare, profusely illustrated 1846 catalog includes Union Army uniform and dress regulations, arms and ammunition, coats, insignia, flags, swords, rifles, etc. 226 illustrations. 160pp. 9 x 12. 24939-5

WOMEN'S FASHIONS OF THE EARLY 1900s: An Unabridged Republication of "New York Fashions, 1909," National Cloak & Suit Co. Rare catalog of mail-order fashions documents women's and children's clothing styles shortly after the turn of the century. Captions offer full descriptions, prices. Invaluable resource for fashion, costume historians. Approximately 725 illustrations. 128pp. 8⅜ x 11¼. 27276-1

THE 1912 AND 1915 GUSTAV STICKLEY FURNITURE CATALOGS, Gustav Stickley. With over 200 detailed illustrations and descriptions, these two catalogs are essential reading and reference materials and identification guides for Stickley furniture. Captions cite materials, dimensions and prices. 112pp. 6½ x 9¼. 26676-1

EARLY AMERICAN LOCOMOTIVES, John H. White, Jr. Finest locomotive engravings from early 19th century: historical (1804–74), main-line (after 1870), special, foreign, etc. 147 plates. 142pp. 11⅜ x 8¼. 22772-3

THE TALL SHIPS OF TODAY IN PHOTOGRAPHS, Frank O. Braynard. Lavishly illustrated tribute to nearly 100 majestic contemporary sailing vessels: Amerigo Vespucci, Clearwater, Constitution, Eagle, Mayflower, Sea Cloud, Victory, many more. Authoritative captions provide statistics, background on each ship. 190 black-and-white photographs and illustrations. Introduction. 128pp. 8⅞ x 11¾. 27163-3

CATALOG OF DOVER BOOKS

THE STORY OF THE TITANIC AS TOLD BY ITS SURVIVORS, Jack Winocour (ed.). What it was really like. Panic, despair, shocking inefficiency, and a little hero-ism. More thrilling than any fictional account. 26 illustrations. 320pp. 5⅜ x 8½.
20610-6

FAIRY AND FOLK TALES OF THE IRISH PEASANTRY, William Butler Yeats (ed.). Treasury of 64 tales from the twilight world of Celtic myth and legend: "The Soul Cages," "The Kildare Pooka," "King O'Toole and his Goose," many more. Introduction and Notes by W. B. Yeats. 352pp. 5⅜ x 8½.
26941-8

BUDDHIST MAHAYANA TEXTS, E. B. Cowell and others (eds.). Superb, accu-rate translations of basic documents in Mahayana Buddhism, highly important in his-tory of religions. The Buddha-karita of Asvaghosha, Larger Sukhavativyuha, more. 448pp. 5⅜ x 8½.
25552-2

ONE TWO THREE . . . INFINITY: Facts and Speculations of Science, George Gamow. Great physicist's fascinating, readable overview of contemporary science: number theory, relativity, fourth dimension, entropy, genes, atomic structure, much more. 128 illustrations. Index. 352pp. 5⅜ x 8½.
25664-2

EXPERIMENTATION AND MEASUREMENT, W. J. Youden. Introductory man-ual explains laws of measurement in simple terms and offers tips for achieving accu-racy and minimizing errors. Mathematics of measurement, use of instruments, exper-imenting with machines. 1994 edition. Foreword. Preface. Introduction. Epilogue. Selected Readings. Glossary. Index. Tables and figures. 128pp. 5⅜ x 8½.   40451-X

DALÍ ON MODERN ART: The Cuckolds of Antiquated Modern Art, Salvador Dalí. Influential painter skewers modern art and its practitioners. Outrageous evaluations of Picasso, Cézanne, Turner, more. 15 renderings of paintings discussed. 44 calligraphic decorations by Dalí. 96pp. 5⅜ x 8½. (Available in U.S. only.)   29220-7

ANTIQUE PLAYING CARDS: A Pictorial History, Henry René D'Allemagne. Over 900 elaborate, decorative images from rare playing cards (14th–20th centuries): Bacchus, death, dancing dogs, hunting scenes, royal coats of arms, players cheating, much more. 96pp. 9¼ x 12¼.
29265-7

MAKING FURNITURE MASTERPIECES: 30 Projects with Measured Drawings, Franklin H. Gottshall. Step-by-step instructions, illustrations for constructing hand-some, useful pieces, among them a Sheraton desk, Chippendale chair, Spanish desk, Queen Anne table and a William and Mary dressing mirror. 224pp. 8⅛ x 11¼.
29338-6

THE FOSSIL BOOK: A Record of Prehistoric Life, Patricia V. Rich et al. Profusely illustrated definitive guide covers everything from single-celled organisms and dinosaurs to birds and mammals and the interplay between climate and man. Over 1,500 illustrations. 760pp. 7½ x 10⅛.
29371-8

Paperbound unless otherwise indicated. Available at your book dealer, online at **www.doverpublications.com**, or by writing to Dept. GI, Dover Publications, Inc., 31 East 2nd Street, Mineola, NY 11501. For current price information or for free catalogues (please indicate field of interest), write to Dover Publications or log on to **www.doverpublications.com** and see every Dover book in print. Dover publishes more than 500 books each year on science, elementary and advanced mathematics, biology, music, art, literary history, social sciences, and other areas.